Writing Windows Device Drivers

By

Y. P. Kanetkar

BPB PUBLICATIONS
B-14, CONNAUGHT PLACE, NEW DELHI-110001

FIRST EDITION 2005 REPRINTED 2016

Distributors:

MICRO BOOK CENTRE
2, City Centre, CG Road,
Near Swastic Char Rasta,
AHMEDABAD-380009 Phone: 26421611

COMPUTER BOOK CENTRE
12, Shrungar Shopping Centre, M.G. Road,
BANGALORE-560001 Phone: 5587923, 5584641

MICRO BOOKS
Shanti Niketan Building, 8, Camac Street,
KOLKATTA-700017 Phone: 22826518, 22826519

BUSINESS PROMOTION BUREAU
8/1, Ritchie Street, Mount Road,
CHENNAI-600002 Phone: 28410796, 28550491

DECCAN AGENCIES
4-3-329, Bank Street,
HYDERABAD-500195
Phone: 24756400, 24756967

MICRO MEDIA
Shop No. 5, Mahendra Chambers, 150 D.N. Road,
Next to Capital Cinema V.T. (C.S.T.) Station,
MUMBAI-400001 Ph.: 22078296, 22078297

BPB PUBLICATIONS
B-14, Connaught Place, NEW DELHI-110001
Phone: 23325760, 23723393, 23737742

INFO TECH
G-2, Sidhartha Building, 96 Nehru Place,
NEW DELHI-110019
Phone: 26438245, 26415092, 26234208

INFO TECH
Shop No. 2, F-38, South Extension Part-1
NEW DELHI-110049
Phone: 24691288, 24641941

BPB BOOK CENTRE
376, Old Lajpat Rai Market,
DELHI-110006 PHONE: 23861747

Introduction

KICIT has been regularly conducting the course titled "Writing Windows Device Drivers" at several software development houses in and outside India. This book contains the material that is used in this course. The material is divided into 10 chapters whose contents are described below in brief.

Chapter 1: Introduction To Device Drivers

The purpose of this chapter is to give the student the minimal amount of knowledge to be able to successfully build a NT 4.0 style device driver. This includes the discussion of NT OS architecture; protection mechanisms provided by the processor etc. NT 4.0 style driver is deliberately taken so that the initial length of the device driver code does not exceed few lines. The student can then quickly focus on building and deploying the driver. The example program provided is compared with a minimal application program to demonstrate how device driver program is different from an application program.

Once the minimal driver is build successfully the chapter covers building a driver that actually accesses a real hardware. Further chapters incrementally build on the concepts discussed in this chapter to build a WDM compliant driver for Windows 2000 / XP.

Chapter 2: Kernel Mode Programming

The chapter covers some more device driver programs. These device driver programs are not strictly device drivers because they do not serve any device but are more appropriately kernel mode programs.

One of the biggest differences between application programs and device drivers is that device drivers cannot make use of console

I/O function to produce output to the screen. They need to make use of debugging services to pass messages to the kernel debugger. The chapter discusses such a kernel mode program.

The chapter also discusses static and dynamic drivers. Static driver are those that get loaded along with the OS and remain loaded till the end of the session consume precious memory. Dynamic drivers on the other hand are loaded on demand and can be unload before requiring a system restart. The chapter focuses on building a bare minimal dynamic driver and a client program that loads / unloads the driver.

Chapter 3: The Windows Driver Model

This chapter focuses on building WDM compliant driver by getting one more step closer to the WDM model. The chapter discusses the mechanism whereby application program's request reach device drivers. This includes understanding some of the architectural aspects of the NT OS such as the HAL, Kernel and the Executive, the Object manager etc.

This chapter also discusses a very important concept of how application software is able to get correctly connected with the appropriate device driver and how this is facilitated by file, driver and device objects and symbolic link objects.

Chapter 4: Communication Between Application And Driver

This chapter goes one step further than the previous and discusses how application software can read / write (communicate) with devices under Windows NT. The chapter builds a driver for a virtual loop back device. A client application writes some bytes to this virtual loop back device. The device driver receives the request from the client and store the bytes sent by the client in its internal buffer. When the client program makes a read request form the device the device driver returns a copy of its internal buffer back to the client. Thus reading and writing mechanism is fully demonstrated.

Chapter 5: Hardware Basics

To be able to write a driver for a real (physical) device one needs to understand the hardware environment of devices. This includes understanding many vital concepts like Memory mapped and I/O mapped address spaces, interrupt mechanisms, etc. The chapter serves as a foundation for the next chapter that involves writing a driver for real (physical) interrupting device.

Chapter 6: Building Real World Drivers

The chapter focuses on building a driver for a parallel port loop back device. This involves building a Programmed I/O driver. While building the driver many important system mechanisms are discussed. Some of these mechanisms include Handling Device Interrupts, Deferred Procedure Calls, Sync Critical Routine, Queuing I/O Request Packets using default serialization mechanism provided by I/O manager.

Chapter 7: Bus Architectures

The chapter discusses the architecture of various buses in existence like ISA, PCI, USB etc and the impact they have on device driver development. The chapter presents a brief overview of these buses and then discusses topics like plug and play support, interrupting and data transfer mechanisms supported by each of these buses.

Chapter 8: USB Drivers

The chapter focuses on the USB bus and building device drivers for the USB bus. The chapter begins by discusses the architecture and the data flow model in the USB. A minimal function driver for a USB device is discussed in the chapter.

Chapter 9: Divers Installation

WDM drivers are installed via an INF text file. The INF file contains script like instructions for controlling the installation operations of a device driver. The chapter discusses the structure of the INF file and the various sections and directives commonly used in an INF file. The chapter also introduces a GENINF tool in the DDK that is used to create a production quality INF file.

Chapter 10: Driver Testing and Debugging

The chapter discusses the very important aspect of device driver development i.e. testing and debugging. Device drivers being a trusted part of the OS are not restricted in any way they can access any memory location and access any hardware they want. Moreover, exceptions that occur in a device driver are not caught by the OS and thus a device driver can easily end up with system crash.

By introducing the topic of testing and debugging such problems are taken care of. For example the chapter shows what happens when the system crashes and how to interpret the contents of the crash screen and the corresponding crash dump file in order to find the reason of the crash. The chapter also discuses the tools and environment required for debugging drivers that can be used for fixing the bugs in the device drivers.

System Requirements

The programs in this book have been tested on Windows 2000 Professional only although it should work on Windows 2000 Server and on Windows XP.

you would need two machines one for executing the driver (target m/c) and another for debugging (host m/c).

The following software is required on the target machine:
- Windows 2000 Professional
- Visual C++ 6.0 Professional
- Microsoft Windows 2000 DDK

The following software is required on each of the host machine.
- Windows 2000 Professional
- Microsoft WinDbg Debugger
- Matching Symbols for Windows 2000 Professional

Apart from these a digital multi-meter would be required for checking voltage on the parallel port connector.

CD Contents

All the programs developed in this book as well as answers to the Labs at the end of each chapter are furnished on the CD in the source code form. For each chapter there is a separate folder on the CD.

Contents

Chapter 1: Introduction To Device Drivers 1

Getting Started 3
Communicating with Devices 4
Parallel Port Device 5
Interaction With Parallel Port 6
What Is A Device Driver? 11
Other Types Of Drivers 15
Road Map To Writing Device Drivers 18
Windows API 20
Programs And Threads 23
Programs And Processes 24
Characteristics of NT based OS 26
Multitasking 27
Multithreading 28
Thread Context 29
Thread Context Switching 32
Pre-emptive Multitasking 33
Multiprocessing 34
Symmetric Multiprocessing 35
Portability 36
Multiple OS Emulation 41
Protection Mechanisms 43
Hardware Privilege Levels 44
Privileged Levels in Intel Processors 45
NT's Use of Privileged Levels 47

Protection Between Applications 50
Hardware Access 51
Hardware Access Under NT 52
Kernel Mode Vs User Mode 54
Device Driver Development 55
Building A Minimal Driver Using DDK 56
Create C Program 57
The DriverEntry Routine 58
Create makefile 59
Creating Sources File 61
Building The Driver 63
Deploying Driver 65
Testing The Driver 67
Accessing Hardware 68
Summary 70
Lab 1A 71
Lab 1B 73

Chapter 2: Kernel Mode Programming 75

A "Hello World" Driver 77
User Mode Vs Kernel Debuggers 80
Remote debugging 82
Preparing for Remote Debugging 83
Establishing Remote Debugging Session 84
Setting BreakPoints 86
Debugging Services 88
DriverEntry( ) Parameters 89
Objects in NT 91
Advantages Of Objects 94
Object Handles 96
Driver Objects 98
WDM drivers 99
Static Vs. Dynamic Drivers 102
Client Application 104
Building the Client 105

Opening Connection with SCM 106
Loading the Driver 107
Starting the Service 111
Unloading The Driver 112
Closing Connection with SCM 114
Testing the Driver 115
Summary 116
Lab 2A 117
Lab 2B 118

Chapter 3: Windows Driver Model 121

Getting Started 123
NT OS Architecture 124
Dispatching Application Requests 129
The IO Subsystem 130
The Object Manager 131
Object Manager's Namespace 132
Writing Driver For Virtual Device 137
Communication With Driver 138
Client For Accessing Virtual Device 145
Opening A Device Connection 146
Terminating Connection with Device 148
Driver For Virtual Device 149
Extending Device Object Structure 150
The DriverEntry( ) Routine 152
Registering Dispatch Routines 153
Creating Device Object 156
Creating Symbolic Link Object 160
Unloading The Driver 163
Object Relationships 164
Handling Create Request 165
Handling the Close Request 170
Testing The Driver 172
Summary 173
Lab 3A 175

Lab 3B 176

Chapter 4: Comm. Between App And Device Driver 177

Getting Started 179
Memory Management 180
Virtual Memory 181
Address Space Layout 183
Translating Virtual Address 186
Demand Based Virtual Memory 190
Paging 191
Reading & Writing From Devices 193
Buffered I/O Technique 195
Layered Driver Model 199
Virtual Loop Back Driver Client 203
Opening Connection with LB Device 204
Writing Data to LB Device 205
Reading Data From VLB Device 207
Writing The VLB Driver 208
DriverEntry( ) Routine 209
Write Dispatch Routine 212
Read Dispatch Routine 218
Close Dispatch Routine 220
Summary 222
Lab 4 223

Chapter 5: Hardware Basics 225

Getting Started 227
Connection With Devices 229
Device Registers 233
Device Register Mapping 236
Memory Mapped I/O 237
Port Mapped I/O 239
Memory Vs. Port Mapped I/O 242
Device Register Addressing 245

Trap 246
Interrupts 248
Exceptions 249
Reasons For Trap 250
Device Signaling 254
Signaling Priority 256
Interrupt Handling 259
Interrupt Priorities 267
IRQL Levels 268
Data Transfer Techniques 274
Hardware Resources 278
Summary 281
Lab 5 282

Chapter 6: Building Real World Drivers 283

Recap 285
More Device Driver Routines 287
The Parallel Port Device 292
Pin Assignments 294
Device Register To Pin Mapping 296
Parallel Port Loop Back Device 297
Interaction With Loop Back Device 303
Code Example 309
String Handling 310
Registering Entry Points 311
AddDevice Routine 313
Handling PnP notifications 325
Passing IRPs Down The Stack 328
Starting The Device 330
Registering ISR 336
Stopping The Device 339
Removing The Device 340
Handling Write Request 342
Cancel( ) Routine 345
Start I/O Routine 346

Transmitting Bytes 349
Handling Interrupts 355
Completing The Request 358
Deploying The Driver 360
Testing The Driver 363
Summary 364
Lab 6 366

Chapter 7: Bus Architectures 369

Overview Of Bus 371
Bus Architectures 375
Hardware Resources Conflicts 376
Resolving Conflicts 378
Plug and Play 379
Interrupt Signaling 386
Hardware Enumeration 391
ISA Bus 393
EISA Bus 401
PCI Bus 408
USB Bus 411
Summary 414
Lab 7 416

Chapter 8: USB Drivers 417

Getting Started 419
USB Device Connection 420
USB Device 423
Layered Communication 426
USB Data Flow Model 429
Auto Recognition Support 434
Device Addressing 436
Writing A USB Driver 437
Code Example 441
Handling PnP 442

Starting The Device 444
Stopping The Device 451
Sending URB To Bus Driver 452
Building The Driver 457
Deploying The Driver 458
Summary 460
Lab 8 462

Chapter 9: Driver Installation 465

Getting Started 467
Providing The INF File 469
Structure Of INF File 470
Syntax Rules For INF Files 474
The Version Section 481
The Manufacturer Section 490
The Models Section 491
Hardware ID Formats 492
Device Identification 499
The Install Section 500
Creating The Driver Service 504
Tools for INF File 514
Summary 517
Lab 9 518

Chapter 10: Driver Testing and Debugging 521

Getting Started 523
WHQL Certification 524
Checked Vs. Free Build OS 527
Checked Build OS 531
Driver Verifier 534
Testing Drivers 545
Driver Debug Environment 546
H/W & S/W Requirements 548
Debug Symbol Files 555

System Crash 560
Analyzing the Crash Dump File 569
Enabling Debug Client 571
Modifying Boot.INI 572
Debugging Routines 577
Summary 581
Lab 10 582

Chapter 1

Introduction To Device Drivers

1

Introduction To Device Drivers

Objectives

After completing this unit you will be able to:

- Understand what exactly a Device Driver is.

- Understand the roadmap for learning Device Driver programming.

- Understand the foundation concepts required to begin Device Driver programming.

- Write a minimal Device Driver and deploy it.

- Write a Device Driver that access hardware.

Getting Started

- The need for writing a device driver can be better understood through a practical example.

- Let us say that we wish to interact with the parallel port device. We would try to write some value to the parallel port device. This value would appear as an electrical signal (+5 volts) on one of the pins of the parallel port connector.

- But before we begin let us try to get hold of the parallel port device itself.

Communicating with Devices

- Locations within a device are known as device registers. These locations can be read or written to by software programs.

- Device registers help the software program to transfer data to / from the device (data register), obtain status of the device (status register) and to control the behavior of the device (control register).

- Each device register has a unique address. This address is usually known as port address.

Parallel Port Device

- The parallel port device has 3 device registers – data, status and control.

- The data register is usually located at the address 378h. The individual bits of the 8bit data register is further mapped to the pins (pin 2 – 9) of a 25 pin female connector found at the back of the CPU box.

- By writing values in the data register one can produce corresponding electrical signals on the pins.

- A bit value of 1 produces a +5V on the corresponding pin and a bit value of 0 produces a +0V.

Interaction With Parallel Port

- DOS is single tasking operating system and hence DOS applications can directly access device registers of any device.

- Given below is a program that writes a value of 0 to the data register of the parallel port device, waits for a key press and then again writes a value of 1 which would result in a +5V to appear on pin number 2.

- See *Chap01\DOS* directory on the CD.

```
# include <dos.h>
void main( )
{
    /* turn off bit 0 */
    outportb ( 0x378, 0 ) ;
    getch( ) ;
    /* turn on bit 0 */
    outportb ( 0x378, 1 ) ;
}
```

- The *outportb( )* function writes values to the specified device register.

- This output can be verified using a Digital Multimeter. Alternatively one can also use the circuit shown in the following figure. When we execute the program the LED in the circuit would glow.

Interaction With Parallel Port

(Cont'd)

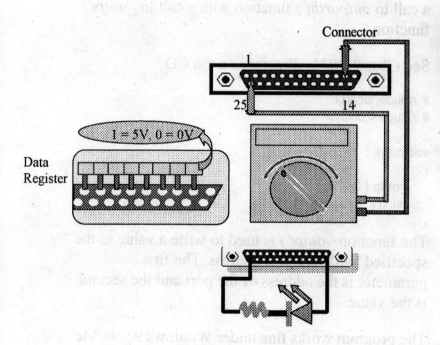

Windows Equivalent

- A equivalent Windows program for interacting with the parallel port device would require us to replace a call to *outportb( )* function with a call to *_outp( )* function.

- See *Chap01\R3Io* directory on the CD.

```
# include "stdafx.h"
# include <conio.h>

void main( )
{
    _outp ( 0x378, 1 ) ;
    printf ( "sucess!\n" ) ;
}
```

- The function *_outp( )* is used to write a value to the specified hardware port address. The first parameter is the address of the port and the second is the value.

- The program works fine under Windows 95/98/Me. However under Window 2000/XP an exception occurs and the program is forced to terminate.

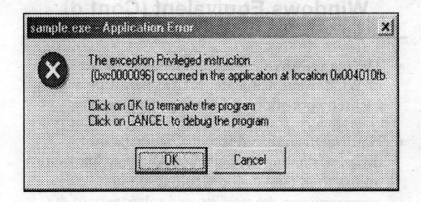

The exception Privileged instruction [0xc0000096] occured in the application at location 0x004010fb.

Click on OK to terminate the program
Click on CANCEL to debug the program

Windows Equivalent (Cont'd)

- The reason why the program fails on NT versions of Windows is that under NT OS hardware access is strictly not allowed from user applications.

- Hardware is a shared resource amongst the different running applications. Allowing hardware access from application would result in compromising the stability and robustness of the OS.

- The only way to solve the problem under NT versions of Windows is by writing a Device Driver.

What Is A Device Driver?

- A device driver is a piece of software that enables a particular hardware device to function (work).

  - Merely connecting the hardware device to the computer and providing it a power supply isn't sufficient for the device to function in any meaningful way.

  - A Device Driver instructs the hardware device to perform different operations.

  - A Device Driver is so named because it drives the operations of the device.

  - Almost all externally or internally connected hardware device requires a Device Driver program for its working.

- Why do we require a separate piece of software for controlling the operations of a hardware device?

  - In a multitasking environment, hardware devices are a shared resource between all the running programs.

  - Allowing hardware access from application program can result in conflict if multiple programs try to access the same device at the same time.

What Is A Device Driver? (Cont'd)

- Why cannot the code for controlling hardware device be an integral part of the OS?

    - Each hardware device internally operates in a different way than another.

    - New hardware devices continue to evolve at a rapid rate.

    - It is not practical to modify, recompile and then redistribute the OS code time and again to accommodate the functionality of new hardware devices.

    - By keeping the code for controlling hardware devices in a separate module the OS remains independent of any particular hardware device.

What Is A Device Driver?

- Device Driver code becomes an extension to the OS

    - The Device Driver program although is a separate piece of program is considered to be a part (actually an extension) to the OS.

    - The OS becomes dynamically extensible by the use of device drivers and thereby manages to run on newer hardware without a need for recompilation.

    - Since Device Driver becomes a part (extension) to the OS it is highly trusted and can do operations normally not allowed from application programs.

    - The figure shows the relationship between application software, OS, device driver and the hardware

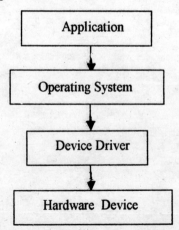

Other Types Of Drivers

- Not every Device Driver program controls a hardware device.

- For example, a File System Driver (FSD) never interacts with any physical hardware.

  - A FSD is responsible for handling file I/O requests from application, converting these requests to a low-level form (Cylinder, Head, Sector request) and passing it to another driver.

  - This 'another' driver actually interacts with the physical storage device.

  - File system drivers bear the responsibility of managing the logical organization of a disk.

  - FSD is required for different types of file systems like FAT, NTFS, CDFS, UDF etc.

Other Types Of Drivers (Cont'd)

- Another utility of driver programs is to write very low-level system code.

  - Drivers are a trusted part of the OS and can do things, which are normally not possible in application level code.

  - System utilities in particular sometimes have an additional module in the form of a driver that performs much of the low-level activities on behalf of the application.

  - For example, monitoring utilities like 'Filemon', which monitors every single disk activities taking place in the system. A client program then displays these activities. The module, which actually logs disk activities, utilizes a driver program at its core.

  - An antiviral software may take help of a driver program to accomplish many of its activities like:
    a) Scanning memory of all running process including the OS.
    b) Proving auto-protect feature whereby any program that is executed is first scanned for

viruses. If a virus is found the antiviral software stops the execution of the program.

- Driver code can also be used to emulate physical hardware devices. For example, there are a lot of commercial and shareware utilities available that can emulate a CD-ROM drive.

Roadmap To Writing Device Drivers

- Drivers for Windows use a variety of architectures and involve understanding of a lot of complicated concepts.

- The proper method to follow when learning Device Drivers programming for Windows platform includes the following:

  - **Learning key Windows concepts** – Device driver is basically an extension to the core OS. Writing device drivers involves coding at the OS level. Hence to successfully learn Device Drivers one must know a lot of concepts and internal mechanisms.

  - **Learn Driver Architecture** – Drivers for Windows follow a very specific architecture. There is a well-defined interface for an application to communicate with a device driver program. Again, when the OS has to communicate with the Device Driver it follows a different packet driven model to do so.

  - **Learn hardware details** – Last but not the least, to actually write driver one has to know the basics of the hardware environment. This includes topics such as device registers, mapping of device registers, accessing hardware device registers in an architecture independent manner, etc.

Windows API

- Windows API facilitates consistent programming across different OS versions.

  - While programming under Windows the programmer directly or indirectly makes use of what is known as the API (Application Programming Interface).

  - API is a group of functions supported by the OS that helps the programmer to build applications.

  - API functions cover a wide variety of areas like processes, threads, memory management, security, I/O, windowing, graphics and so on.

  - API for Windows remains pretty consistent when it comes to programming the different versions of Windows.

- The implementation of API functions differs between the different versions of Windows OS.

  - The API functions are implemented in three DLLs, namely **GDI32.DLL**, **USER32.DLL** and **KERNEL32.DLL**.

  - Most of the API functions inside these DLLs do not contain the actual implementation logic and simply delegate the execution control to some other component of the OS.

− The sizes of the three DLLs turn out to be few hundred kilobytes since the actual logic for the API functions is present in separate modules.

Windows API (Cont'd)

- The following table shows the names of the files that contain the actual implementation of the API functions along with their file sizes.

Component	DLL	Windows 2000 Implementation File
Drawing & Painting	GDI32.DLL (229 KB)	WIN32K.SYS (1.65MB)
Windowing	USER32.DLL (393KB)	WIN32K.SYS (1.65MB)
All others	KERNEL32.DLL (715 KB)	NTOSKRNL.EXE (1.63 MB)

- The three DLLs form a consistent interface for calling functions within the OS, whereas the actual implementation is quite separate from the interface and is physically stored in a separate file.

- This facilitates the implementation code to change from one version of OS to another without affecting application programs.

Programs And Threads

- A program is a sequence of instructions that would get executed when loaded in memory.

- A thread is a unit of program execution.

  - This unit is usually a function/subroutine within the program.

  - Every running program at least has one such unit (thread) that executes the program. This thread is often known as the main thread.

  - Execution of a program begins with the main thread.

  - The main thread can then create additional threads.

  - Multiple threads within a program allow for the simultaneous execution of two or more parts of the same program.

Programs And Processes

- The OS represents a single running program by creating a process for it.

  - A program is not same as a process.

  - A process is a container for all the threads of a program and the set of resources used by those threads.

  - These resources include the memory required for all the threads, list of handles to kernel-mode objects (objects and handles are discussed later), security context for the program and so on.

- When a program is executed a process containing a single thread (main thread) would be launched in memory.

  - This main thread in turn may launch several more threads.

- A process is often termed as an inen. object.

  - The process is not a unit of program execution and hence no time slots are allocated for a process in a multitasking environment.

  - Time slots are allocated on a per thread basis.

- If there are several processes running in memory each housing several threads then all the threads of all the processes would get time-slots in an order decided by the thread scheduler.

Characteristics of NT based OS

- Any NT based OS enjoys the following major characteristics:

  - Multitasking

  - Multithreading

  - Multiprocessing

  - Portability

  - Multiple OS Emulation

Multitasking

- As its name suggests, it is a mechanism whereby more than one task executes simultaneously.

- This is achieved by rapidly switching among the units of execution, allowing each to run for a short period of time. This characteristic of the OS is termed as multitasking.

- For some OS a process is a unit of execution (Ex. Unix), whereas for some a thread is a unit of executions (Ex. Windows).

Multithreading

- Under NT the unit of execution is a thread and hence multiple threads (of the same or different process) run simultaneously.

- The activity, which involves deciding the next thread that is to be run, is technically referred as thread scheduling.

  - Thread scheduling is almost entirely based on the priority of the thread.

  - Each thread has its own scheduling priority.

  - The OS does not take into consideration the process to which a thread belongs when it makes scheduling decisions.

  - The OS as multitasking part of its responsibilities allocates time slices to all threads depending upon their priority value.

  - The type of multitasking where threads instead of processes are given time slices is often referred to as multithreading.

Thread Context

- The microprocessor has a set of temporary locations within itself that are known as registers.

  - These registers play an important role in the execution of instructions.

  - Any mathematical or logical operations cannot be done directly on the data stored in the memory.

  - The data has to be firstly brought from the memory into the registers. Any temporary results generated would also get stored within the registers. And finally, the results of the operations are copied from these registers to the memory.

  - Registers are also useful for addressing memory locations, holding loop counter values and so on.

  - So almost every single instruction of a program ends up makes use of registers in some way or the other.

  - As the instructions execute the value of the various registers gets modified.

- CPU registers are a shared resource of the system. There is only a single set of registers in the microprocessor.

Thread Context (Cont'd)

- A thread is an independent path of execution unit within a program.

  - The execution of one thread does not have any side effects on the execution of another thread.

  - When the OS switches from one thread to another as a part of multithreading the CPU register values would have to saved onto some memory location.

  - This is because the other thread would certain modify the values of registers and then when it is time to return back to the first thread the first thread would find unexpected values in the registers.

  - A threads context also contains all the information apart from the CPU registers that has to be preserved onto the stack such that the thread switching does not have any side effects on the execution of any of the threads.

- A thread's context and the procedure for context switching vary depending on the processor's architecture

Thread Context Switching

- A typical context switch requires saving and reloading the following data:

  - Program counter / Instruction Pointer register

  - Processor status register

  - Other register contents

  - **User and kernel stack pointers** - Each running thread has two stacks one for user mode and another for kernel mode. When the thread enters the kernel mode the kernel mode stack is used and when the thread executes in user mode the user mode stack is used.

  - A pointer to the address space in which the thread runs

Pre-emptive Multitasking

- When a thread is selected to run, it is scheduled to run for a time-period called a quantum.

  - The quantum value indicates the maximum length of time the thread will be allowed to run before another thread is scheduled.

- While a given thread is running, if a high priority thread becomes ready to run, then the lower priority thread is stopped from running and the higher priority thread is started.

  - If the thread runs for its entire quantum, the system pre-empts (takes over) the thread from running and selects a new thread to run.

  - This type of multitasking is known as pre-emptive multitasking

- Even if one thread does not give up the control after its quantum has expired (because the thread has possible stuck up inside an infinite loop), the OS forcibly takes away the execution control away from the errant thread.

  - This is necessary in order to guarantee that the other threads do get a chance to execute.

Multiprocessing

- Multitasking is the OS technique for sharing a single processor among multiple threads of execution.

- When a computer has more than one processor, however, it can actually execute two or more threads simultaneously.

  - Thus, whereas a multitasking OS only appears to execute multiple threads at the same time, a multiprocessing OS actually does it, executing one thread on each of its processors.

- There are two types of multiprocessing system

  - Symmetric multiprocessing (SMP) and

  - Asymmetric multiprocessing (ASMP).

- NT OS follows the SMP model.

Symmetric Multiprocessing

- The OS as well as all user application threads can be scheduled to run on any processor.

  - Under SMP there is no master processor

  - All the processors share one memory space.

  - Interrupt signals from device can also target any of the available microprocessors.

  - In other words all the processors in an SMP system are treated equally.

  - This model contrasts with ASMP, in which the OS typically selects one processor (master processor) to execute OS code while other processors run only user code.

  - The master processor is alone responsible for handling all the interrupts from the devices.

  - The number of processor that NT supports largely depends upon the version and edition of the OS.

  - Windows 2000 Professional supports 2 processors while Windows 2000 Server edition supports 4 processors.

Portability

- One of the benefits of an NT based OS is that it is portable across a variety of processor architectures.

  - NT is designed to run on a variety of hardware architectures, including Intel-based CISC (Complex Instruction set computing) systems as well as RISC (Reduced Instruction Set Computing) systems.

- Portability is achieved in two primary ways:

  - Layered Design

  - Use of C Language

- Layered Design

  - NT uses a layered design, in which the low-level portions of the system are processor-architecture specific or platform-specific.

  - These low-level portions are also isolated into separate modules so that upper-layers of the system can be shielded from the differences between architectures and among hardware platforms.

- In NT, the kernel and HAL (Hardware Abstraction Layer) contain architecture specific code.

- The kernel is packaged into as separate mode namely ntoskrnl.exe whereas the HAL is present in a separate module **hal.dll**.

Portability (Cont'd)

- – Functions that are architecture-specific such as thread context switching and Trap dispatching are implemented in the kernel.

- – Functions that can differ among systems within the same architecture for example, differences in motherboards are implemented in the HAL.

- • Use of C language

  - – The C language compilers are available for almost all processor architectures.

  - – This makes code written in C language to be portable across different architectures.

  - – To be able to port the code for a new platform one has to recompile the source code of the program using an appropriate compiler for the target platform.

  - – It is the use of C language, which helps NT's upper layers to remain portable across different processor architectures.

  - – A major portion of NT is written in C, with some portions in C++.

 − Assembly language is used only for those parts
   of the OS that need to communicate directly
   with system hardware or that are extremely
   performance-sensitive (such as thread context
   switching).

Portability (Cont'd)

- The Executive part of NT largely remains portable

  - The various components of the OS (excluding the kernel and the HAL) like process and thread manager, memory manger, cache manger, object manager etc. are collectively referred to as the Executive.

  - The Executive, Kernel and HAL constitute the major parts of the NT OS and they all run in kernel mode.

  - The Executive largely remains portable because the kernel and HAL shield the executive from the architecture specific details of the system.

  - A very large portion of the executive is written in C.

Multiple OS Emulation

- NT supports execution of Win32, POSIX, OS/2, DOS and Windows 3.1 programs.

  - To achieve the target of supporting varies types of programs NT OS emulates the corresponding OS environment.

- Environment Subsystem is an independent user mode process that emulates the behavior of a specific OS.

  - For example the Win32 Environment subsystem is basically a process CSRSS.EXE (Client Server Runtime Sub-System) running in user mode that helps emulate the Windows OS to run 32 bit Windows programs.

  - Similarly NT also has an OS/2 (**os2.exe**) and POSIX (Portable operating system interface) **psxss.exe** environment subsystems.

  - An Environment Subsystem exports the API for the OS that it emulates.

  - An application program can only uses one environments system at a time.

- As a result of which, application programs cannot make API calls into another environment subsystem.

Protection Mechanisms

- It is highly necessary for the OS to be as robust and stable as possible.

  - For example an errant or buggy program should not be able to bring the OS down.

  - Also one running application shouldn't be able to effect another running application.

- Application programs should not be allowed access to the code and data of the OS.

  - This clearly demands for the monitoring of memory access made by the running application programs and denying the access if necessary.

  - If the OS were to monitor this itself then the overall execution speed of the entire system would suffer heavily.

  - To help solve this problem all modern microprocessor provide protection mechanism as a part of the hardware itself.

Hardware Privilege Levels

- Microprocessors provide protection mechanisms by implementing what are known as privileged levels.

  - These privileged levels are nothing more than code execution levels.

  - Every single piece of code that is running on the system executes at one level or another.

  - A code running at a lower privilege level (code execution level) cannot access the memory (code and data) of another program whose code is running at a high privileged level thus providing a protection mechanism.

  - If such an attempt is ever made the processor raises an exception, which results in the termination of the errant program (that access the memory).

  - However the reverse is true the code running at higher privileged level can easily access all the memory of the program running at a lower privileged level.

Privileged Levels in Intel Processors

- The Intel microprocessor provides four privileged levels numbered from 0 to 3.

- Under the Intel's terminology these privileged levels are termed as rings.

  - Ring 3 (or privileged level 3) happens to be the least privileged level whereas Ring 0 (or privileged level 0) is the most privileged level).

  - Intel suggests that the OS developers should use the four levels as illustrated below so as to guarantee a more robust operating system.

Ring / Privileged Level	Component to be run
0	Kernel
1	Device Drivers
2	File System Driver
3	Application Programs

- Under this scheme, for example a device driver
  program cannot access the memory of the kernel
  program or an application program cannot
  access the memory of any of the file system
  driver, device driver of the kernel.

NT's Use of Privileged Levels

- Not all microprocessors architectures implement a four- privileged level scheme.

  - Every microprocessor at the minimum, implements at least two such privileged levels.

- NT based OSs, only make use of two levels Ring 0 (most privileged level) and Ring 3 (least privileged level).

  - NT does this so as to remain portable across different microprocessor architectures

  - NT runs all the OS and device driver code at Ring 0 and all the application programs at Ring 3.

  - Thus it is not possible for an application running under NT to access and thereby possibly corrupt the memory of the OS or device driver.

- Because the word 'Ring' happens to be specific to the Intel architecture NT uses a different terminology to refer them.

  - NT uses the term 'Kernel-Mode' to refer to the most privileged level of any processor architecture and the term 'User-Mode' to refer to the least privileged level of any processor architecture.

NT's Use of Privileged Levels

(Cont'd)

- Device driver code and OS code execute at the same privileged level i.e. Ring 0 or most privileged level.

  - A buggy device driver can very easily corrupt the OS.

- This is one of the reasons why Microsoft stresses on the digital signing of Device Drivers.

  - Digitally signed drivers are the drivers which have passed a thorough test from Microsoft's labs and are guaranteed that they won't cause the OS to misbehave or stop functioning.

Protection Between Applications

- As said earlier all application programs run at the same privileged level.

  - Hence an application could very easily corrupt or effect the execution of another application.

  - The OS uses a different strategy to prevent this from happening.

- The memory manger component of the OS is responsible for this protection.

  - NT achieves protection amongst running application programs by strictly controlling the memory usage of each application.

Hardware Access

- Hardware access involves reading/writing from/to the memory locations present in a hardware device.

  - This mainly involves performing port input/output. (See chapter Hardware basics for a through explanation of ports and port input/output).

- Program running under DOS could easily perform port input /output operation and manage to access the hardware device.

  - Under MS-DOS OS only one program could run at a given time and the program was in the complete control of the machine.

Hardware Access Under NT

- Under NT OS applications cannot directly access hardware by performing port input / output

  - NT is a multitasking OS under which many programs may be running simultaneously.

  - Now if two or more such running applications try to access the same device at the same time then surely this is a problem since hardware is a shared resource.

  - To solve this problem the port input/output instruction is made a privileged instruction.

  - Privileged instructions can only be executed by code running at kernel mode (most privileged level).

  - Hence application programs cannot execute any of the port input/output instructions and as a result of which application programs cannot directly access hardware device.

  - Privileged instructions often modify the critical states of the processor that can adversely affect the functioning of the OS.

- Device drivers however execute at kernel mode and hence can easily execute any privileged instructions.

Kernel Mode Vs User Mode

- A program whose code is running at user mode can only access its own memory and cannot execute privileged instructions.

  - Code running at Kernel Mode can access any memory location and can executed any CPU instruction including privileged instructions.

- Most of the OS code runs at kernel mode.

  - User mode applications cannot access or modifying critical OS data.

  - No protection is provided to private read/write system memory being used by components running in kernel mode

  - Once in kernel mode, OS and device driver code has complete access to system space memory and can bypass protection mechanism.

  - Kernel mode components must be carefully designed and tested to ensure that they don't affect system integrity.

Device Driver Development

- Device Driver Development requires Driver Development Kit (DDK) available from Microsoft.

  - DDK contains headers, libraries, tools and documentation required to build device drivers.

  - DDK only offers building device drivers from the command line.

- DDK provides two environments checked build and free build.

  - Checked build is similar to driver debug version

  - Free build is similar to driver release version.

Building A Minimal Driver Using DDK

- Following steps are required to build a minimal Device Driver

    - Create C Program

    - Create makefile for building driver

    - Provide driver specific information - sources

    - Build the driver

    - Deploy the driver

Create C Program

- Every Device Driver program contains a C program at its core.

- A C program for a minimal driver is as below

- See *Chap01\minimal* directory on the CD.

```
/* minimal.c */
# include <wdm.h>

NTSTATUS DriverEntry(IN PDRIVER_OBJECT  pDrvObj, IN
PUNICODE_STRING pRegPath )
{
    return STATUS_SUCCESS ;
}
```

- *wdm.h* is the main header file for Device Drivers

  - **wdm.h** contains definitions for the data types, constants, functions, and macros used in device driver programs

  - WDM in **wdm.h** stands for Window Driver Model – basically a specification for writing drivers that are source compatible with Windows 98/Me and Windows 2000/XP.

The DriverEntry Routine

- Every Device Driver must at least contain a function named *DriverEntry()*.

  - **DriverEntry()** function is not same as **main( )** / **WinMain( )** function of an application.

  - Driver execution does not stop at the end of **DriverEntry()** function.

  - Device Driver programs are event driven i.e. there is no sequential execution of instructions.

  - NTSATUS is a typedef of long it indicates status code for function success, failure etc.

  - The keyword IN is optional and acts as an visual indicator for input parameter

  - **DriverEntry()** function must return STATUS_SUCCESS otherwise the device driver is immediately unloaded from the memory.

  - At this stage we would not bother about the 2 parameters of **DriverEntry()** function

Create makefile

- *Makefile* is a special text file bearing the name "makefile" without any extension

  - This file is required for compiling and linking device driver programs

  - Basically the file is supposed to contain instructions for the compiler (VC++) to compile and link the mentioned files and correctly generate a .sys file for the device driver

  - Because these instructions do not change with every device driver program, Microsoft wrote a makefile for us in the file **makefile.def** present in the DDK installation directory.

  - We have to include the **makefile.def** from within our **makefile**.

- The only line of code required for the *makefile* is

  ```
  !INCLUDE $(NTMAKEENV)\makefile.def
  ```

  - INCLUDE is a directive similar to **#include** in C/C++.

- NTMAKEENV is an environment variable
  which contains the path of the DDK directory
  containing the **makefile.def**.

Creating Sources File

- Because makefile.def requires that we specify additional information in a text file named "sources" without any extension

- The sources file contains various macros along with their values

- At least 4 macros must be specified in the sources file as show

```
TARGETNAME = minimal
TARGETPATH = obj
TARGETTYPE = DRIVER
SOURCES = minimal.c
```

- The macros and their meaning are as under

  - TARGETNAME indicates the filename of the .sys. Note that the name of the .c file does not have any bearing on the name of the final .sys file

  - TARGETPATH specifies a string name used to construct the complete name of the folder which contains intermediate files and the .sys file

- TARGETTYPE specifies what type of output is expected. DRIVER specifies to build a kernel mode driver

- SOURCES specifies a list of source files seperated by spaces or commas that are part of the device driver project

Building The Driver

- Start "Checked Build Environment"

- Change current directory to project directory

- Type build -cZ from the command prompt

  - c and Z indicate command line arguments passed to the build utility

  - c specifies that all intermediate object files (if any) be deleted

  - Z specifies that no dependency checking should be performed , i.e all files would have to be compiled.

- After successfully building the driver the .sys file gets created in the following directory

  - For Checked Build \objchk\i386\minimal.sys

  - Free Build   \objfre\i386\minimal.sys

- Directory names may differ with DDK releases

Deploying Driver

- To deploy the driver we simply create a service entry in the registry.

  - Services are programs that usually do not interact with any logged in user.

  - Services are there to support the system

  - Device Drivers are nothing but services running in kernel mode.

- To automate the process of modifying the registry we need to create a registry script.

  - The registry script file has an .reg extension

  - The file can also be generated by first making the entries manually using the registry editor (regedit.exe) and then saving the registry values to the .reg file.

```
REGEDIT4
[HKEY_LOCAL_MACHINE\System\CurrentContro
lSet\Services\minimal]
"Start" = dword:1
"Type" = dword:1
"DisplayName" = "a minimal driver"
"ErrorControl" = dword:1
```

Deploying Driver (Cont'd)

- The "services" branch contains entries for service like Device Drivers, File System Drivers and Win32 Services programs.

  - Each sub key under the services branch corresponds to a service.

  - Values in the individual keys govern the behavior of the service

- The "Start" value specifies the type of service load method.

  - A 0 value indicates that the service (device driver) is loaded at boot time by the kernel loader

  - A value of 1 indicates that the service is started after the kernel initialization is over.

  - A value of 2 indicates that the service is automatically started by the Service Control Manager (SCM)

  - A value of 3 indicates that the service would not start automatically it would require manual start.

Testing The Driver

- Copy the .sys file of the driver to the %windir%\system32\drivers directory and double click the .reg file.

- Restart the system.

- Right Click MyComputer and select Manage

- From Computer Management select System Tools | System Information | Software Environment | Drivers.

- An entry for the minimal driver can be seen on the right pane.

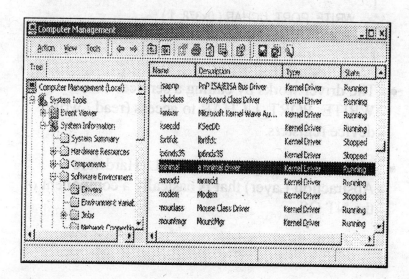

Accessing Hardware

- Here is a device driver that access hardware. The driver sends a value 1 to the data register of the parallel port device.

- No exception however occurs this time since the device driver runs at a more privileged level (kernel mode i.e. ring 0).

- See *Chap01\R0Io* directory on the CD.

```
# include <wdm.h>

NTSTATUS DriverEntry ( PDRIVER_OBJECT pDrvObj,
                       PUNICODE_STRING pRegPath )
{
    WRITE_PORT_UCHAR ( 0x378, 1 ) ;
    return STATUS_SUCCESS ;
}
```

- The driver works by calling a service WRITE_PORT_UCHAR to access (read / write) device registers.

- This service is a part of the HAL (Hardware Abstraction Layer) that is basically a component of the NT OS.

Accessing Hardware (Cont'd)

- This service enables the device driver to access hardware device registers in an architecture independent fashion.

- The first parameter is the address of the device register and the second is the value that needs to be written.

- When the driver loads, the *DriverEntry( )* function gets called and the WRITE_PORT_UCHAR gets called which sends the value 1 to the data register as a result of which +5V appear on the 2nd pin of the parallel port connector.

Summary

- Device Drivers are separate piece of software programs that control the functioning of hardware devices.

- Driver programs are sometimes used to perform low-level system activities that are not possible with application programs.

- Any NT based OS has the following characteristics multitasking, multithreading, multiprocessing, portability and multiple OS emulation.

- Layered Architecture of NT helps in keeping the OS portable across different architectures.

- Every processor provides some kind of protection mechanisms to help the OS in protecting itself from errant applications.

- NT OS uses only 2 levels of protections kernel-mode and user mode.

- Direct hardware access is possible only in kernel-mode.

Lab 1A

Driver Object Structure

Write a device driver that displays the following elements of the driver object structure:

DriverInit – contains the address of the *DriverEntry( )* routine

HardwareDatabase – pointer to the **\Registry\Machine\Hardware** path to the hardware configuration information in the registry.

Suggested time: 30 minutes

Answers Directory: Chap01\drvobj

Files: drvobj.c, makefile, sources, install.reg

Instructions:

• Create the driver program, the source file and the makefile.

• Build the driver and deploy it using a registry script.

• Reboot the system.

- Watch the debug messages in the kernel debugger window.

Lab 1B

DriverEntry Routine

Build a driver that does not return START_SUCESS from *DriverEntry( )* and observer the status of the driver after deploying it.

Suggested time: 20 minutes

Answers Directory: Chap01\drventry

Files: drventry.c, makefile, sources, install.reg

Instructions:

- Create the driver program, the source file and the makefile.

- Make sure that *DriverEntry( )* routine does not return STATUS_SUCCESS value.

- Build the driver and deploy it using a registry script.

- Reboot the system.

- Test the status of the driver from the computer management applet.

Chapter 2

Kernel Mode Programming

Kernel Mode Programming

Objectives

After completing this unit you will be able to:

- Learn how to send messages to kernel debugger.

- Understand Device Driver debugging environment.

- Understand static and dynamic drivers.

A "Hello World" Driver

- Device Drivers are service programs and usually do not directly interact with the end user.

- Device Drivers still require a way to display formatted messages for the following reasons.

  - Displaying messages can easily help to trace the flow of programs execution.

  - It can also help to print diagnostic messages.

- Device Drivers cannot simply use a C runtime library functions like *printf( )* or Windows API functions.

  - The C Runtime library functions and the Windows API functions are not designed to work with kernel mode.

  - Device Drivers can only use the services exported from the kernel or from any other kernel mode OS component.

A "Hello World" Driver (Cont'd)

- Here is a driver that passes some message to the kernel debugger.

- See *Chap02\Hello* directory on the CD.

```
/* hello.c */
# include <wdm.h>

NTSTATUS DriverEntry ( PDRIVER_OBJECT pDrvObj,
                       PUNICODE_STRING pRegPath )
{
    DbgPrint ( "Hello driver: Inside DriverEntry\n" ) ;
    return STATUS_SUCCESS ;
}
```

- *DbgPrint( )* is one of the kernel mode functions that a Device Driver typically uses to display (print) formatted messages to the kernel debugger window.

- The syntax of *DbgPrint( )* function is similar to *printf()* function except that the output goes to the Kernel debugger instead of console.

A "Hello World" Driver (Cont'd)

- *DbgPrint( )* works both in free as well as checked build of OS.

  - OS that we commercially use is free build OS. Free build is similar to release build in VC++.

  - Every single program or DLL within the Free Build OS is optimized for performance or size and usually do not contain debugging information.

  - Microsoft also provides a debug version of its OS known as checked build OS.

  - The name checked indicates that the OS performs a rigorous checking of the parameters passed to the functions of the kernel.

  - If any parameter is not valid then the checked build OS displays the error information and halt the system.

- *KdPrint( )* is similar to *DbgPrint( )* but has no effect in Free build of OS.

- To test the driver we have to use the Kernel Debugger that is the topic of the next section.

User Mode Vs Kernel Debuggers

- Debuggers are of two types user mode debugger and kernel mode debugger

  - User mode debuggers are used to debug application programs.

  - Kernel mode debuggers are used to debug Operating System and Device Driver code.

- Almost all User Mode debugger offer interactive debugging.

  - When using a user mode debugger like VC++ we get interactive debugging support.

  - For example in VC++ pressing keys like F11 can help us to execute the statements of the program one by one.

- Unlike this when debugging kernel mode code no such interactive debugging facility is available.

  - Explicit code has to be written for debugging.

  - This off course makes debugging Device Drivers a little tedious.

- Most of the powerful Kernel mode debuggers run remotely on a different machine.

  - Some kernel mode debuggers support local debugging as well as remote debugging, for example SoftICE.

  - Microsoft provided debugger WinDbg only supports remote debugging.

Remote debugging

- In Remote Debugging the debugger runs on another machine known as host machine.

  - The machine whose code is being debugged is known as target machine.

  - The target and the host machine are connected either through a serial port, 1394 port or modem.

Preparing for Remote Debugging

- Following are the steps required to setup a remote debugging session using WinDbg over serial port.

- Connect the target machine to the host over the COM (Serial) port using a null-modem cable.

  - NULL modem means not really a modem device. Both the computer (target and host) think that they are communicating with a modem device.

- Install WinDbg on the host machine.

- Install Operating System symbols on the host machine.

  - Symbols contain function names, variable names of kernel, HAL, Executive etc.

  - It also contains messages corresponding to error codes, success codes.

- Configure symbol path in WinDbg.

  - This can be accomplished by using **File | Symbol Path** command.

Establishing Remote Debugging
Session

- Start WinDbg on the host machine.

- Select File | Kernel Debug and select OK.

- Boot the target machine in debugging mode.
  - Press F8 during booting of windows 2000 and select "debugging mode" then boot normally.

- As soon as the driver gets loaded *DriveEntry( )* would get called and as a result *DbgPrint( )* would get executed.

- The output appears as shown in the following figure

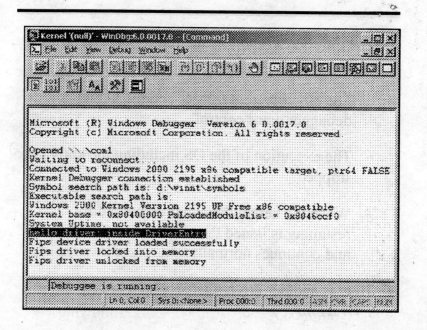

Setting BreakPoints

- The *DbgBreakPoint( )* function executes a break point instruction.

  - The target system freezes and the kernel debugger gains control.

  - The execution of the OS including the kernel is stopped.

  - When the kernel debugger command for resuming is issued the target system unfreezes and continues normally.

- Here is another driver that sets up a breakpoint at *DriverEntry( )*.

- See *Chap02\breakpt* directory on the CD.

```
# include <wdm.h>
NTSTATUS DriverEntry ( PDRIVER_OBJECT  pDrvObj,
PUNICODE_STRING pRegPath)
{
    DbgPrint ( "inside DriverEntry()" ) ;
    DbgBreakPoint( ) ;
    return STATUS_SUCCESS ;
}
```

Setting BreakPoints (Cont'd)

- The WinDbg command for resuming the execution of the target system is G.

  - G indicates go.

  - When we type G on the host machine the WinDbg debugger sends a suitable command over the serial port to indicate the target system to unfreeze and continue with its execution.

- Why is it that the OS freezes even though the breakpoint instruction was only called from the device driver program?

  - Device Driver is basically a part (extension) of OS.

  - Device Driver programs usually modify the state of the OS.

  - It often becomes necessary for us to view the internal state of the OS for successful development of kernel mode code.

Debugging Services

- A few more debugging routines are provided.

  - For example *DbgBreakPointWithStatus( )* can be used to pass a special status (numeric value) to the kernel debugger.

  - *KdBreakPoint( )* and *KdBreakPointWithSatus( )* is similar but only works in checked build of the OS.

  - *ASSERT( )* executes an breakpoint instruction if the condition mentioned in ASSERT fails.

  - *ASSERTMSG( )* is identical to *ASSERT( )*, except that it sends an additional message to the debugger.

DriverEntry( ) Parameters

- The *DriverEntry( )* routine is passed 2 parameters

  - Pointer to a **DRIVER_OBJECT** and

  - Pointer to a **UNICODE_STRING** structure containing the service name in the registry.

- All strings within the kernel mode part of the OS are represented in Unicode.

  - Unicode is represented in kernel mode by a structure known as **UNICODE_STRING**.

- Assuming that the driver is *sample.sys* with a service name of "sample" then what would get passed as the second parameter to *DriverEntry( )* is something similar to

  REGISTRY\MACHINE\SYSTEM\ControlSet001\Services\sample

  - REGISTRY\MACHINE is an alias to HEKY_LOCAL_MACHINE branch of the registry.

  - A ControlSet is the set of configuration that decides what particular drivers or services are required to boot the NT OS.

- Up to 4 different individual control set can be
  defined.

Objects in NT

- NT is object based not object oriented.

  - Every single entity within the OS like process, threads, regions of memory, file, device drivers, fonts, pens and brushes, etc are represented with objects.

  - This object is not same as C++ object. C++ objects are instances of classes.

- NT OS is written almost entirely in the C language, which does not obviously support C++ objects.

  - Objects in NT are instances of structures.

  - An object in NT is a single, run-time instance of a statically defined object type.

  - An object type comprises a system-defined data type, functions that operate on instances of the data type, and a set of object attributes.

  - An object attribute is a field of data in an object that partially defines the object's state.

  - For example process object would have attributes that include the process ID, a base scheduling priority, and so on.

Objects in NT (Cont'd)

- Object methods, are the only means for manipulating objects

- Object methods usually read or change the object attributes.

  - For example, the open method for a process would accept a process identifier as input and return a pointer to the object as output.

- Objects exported (made available) to the programmers from the API and are often known as Executive or User Objects.

  - These objects are further based on lower-level objects that NT creates and manages.

  - Lower-level objects are some times know as kernel objects since they are created by code running in kernel mode.

- The most fundamental difference between an object and an ordinary data structure is that the internal structure of an object is hidden.

  - One must call an object method to retrieve data out of an object or to put data into it.

- This difference separates the underlying implementation of the object from code that merely uses it, a technique that allows object implementations to be changed easily over time.

Advantages Of Objects

- Objects provide a convenient means for accomplishing 4 important OS tasks:

  - Providing human-readable names for system resources

  - Sharing resources and data among processes

  - Protecting resources from unauthorized access

  - Object lifetime management (Reference tracking) - Allows the OS to know when an object is no longer in use so that the memory used by the object can be automatically de-allocated.

- Not all data structures in NT OS are objects.

  - Only data that needs to be shared, protected, named, or made visible to user-mode programs is placed in objects.

  - Structures used by only one component of the OS to implement internal functions are not objects.

- In NT a centralized manager known as object manager is responsible for the management of objects.

    - The management of object involves common things that take care of the object lifetime management and security implementation for the object.

    - Object manager is a subcomponent of the Executive.

Object Handles

- Object handles are numbers used to uniquely refer to an object.

  - An object handle is not same as object pointer

  - Handle is a special encrypted value that cannot be used to reach to the object in memory.

- Whenever an object gets created the NT OS returns back a handle to the application program.

  - When we need to refer to the object we can pass the object handle as a parameter to the API function.

  - NT OS internally maintains a table that correlates handles with their corresponding pointer values.

- Why does NT not return the pointer to the object to user mode programs?

  - It would then open up the possibility that applications can then reach the object and try to corrupt the object.

- – Providing the address of the object would contradict with the implementation hiding of the object.

- • Kernel mode code however makes use of object address rather than the object handle.

Driver Objects

- After every device driver is successfully loaded in memory the I/O manager (subcomponent of the executive) creates a driver object to represent the driver.

- The I/O manager then passes a pointer to the same driver object as the first parameter when it calls the *DriverEntry( )* function

- The Driver object contains many function pointers containing the addresses of the routines that the Device Driver exports.

  - The I/O manager always calls such function by their address and never by their name.

  - All functions except **DriverEntry( )** has to be announced to the OS by setting up the address of functions in the function pointers of the Driver Object.

WDM drivers

- WDM stands for Windows Driver Model.

- WDM is a specification for developing Device Drivers.

- WDM drivers are source compatible between Windows 98/ME and Windows NT family.

- Every WDM driver is a basically a kernel mode program that should additionally support the following features

  - Dynamically loading / unloading.

  - **Consistent interface with clients and OS -** Consistent Interface – Client applications should communicate with Device Drivers using a consistent interface.

  - **Support Plug and Play -** Device Driver should not hardcode any values in the code. They should communicate with the Plug and Play manager to find out the necessary values / addresses of resources. For example although most of the time the address of the data register of the parallel port is found to be 378h a device driver should not hardcode the value in its routines.

- **Events and Error Logging** - Publish configuration and error information via Windows Management Instrumentation (WMI)

- **Layering** – The device driver code should be broken down in different units if possible to form a layer of drivers.

WDM drivers (Cont'd)

- **Hardware Access** - Access hardware only by calling the services of the Hardware Abstraction Layer (HAL) or the lower layered bus drivers

- **Portability** – Device Driver should not use the instructions of a specific type of processor. It should use HAL (hardware abstraction layer services) to access hardware

- **INF Installation** - Device Drivers should be installed via an .INF installation file.

- WHQL requires that drivers should be strictly WDM compliant.

  - Microsoft Windows Hardware Quality Labs (WHQL) tests hardware devices and device drivers.

- Note:

  - Implementing all these features in the very first device driver would make the driver program long and impossible to understand. As we go along we would keep implementing a single feature of the WDM specification so as to ease learning.

Static Vs. Dynamic Drivers

- A driver is known as static Device Driver if it does not implement a Driver Unload routine.

  - Static drivers require a reboot for loading / unloading.

- Dynamic drivers can be loaded / unloaded dynamically at any time.

- The code example below shows a driver that implements the Driver Unload routine.

- See *Chap02\dyndrv* directory on the CD.

```
# include <wdm.h>
NTSTATUS DriverEntry ( PDRIVER_OBJECT  pDrvObj,
PUNICODE_STRING pRegPath )
{
    pDrvObj -> DriverUnload = Unload ;
    DbgPrint ( "Inside DriverEntry\n" ) ;
    return STATUS_SUCCESS ;
}
void Unload (PDRIVER_OBJECT pDrvObj )
{
    DbgPrint ( "Inside Unload\n" ) ;
}
```

Static Vs. Dynamic Drivers (Cont'd)

- *DriverEntry( )* function announces other Entry points by filling in function pointers of the driver object.

- Implementing the *DriverUnload( )* routine makes driver dynamically unloadable.

- Driver Unload function is called when the client requests that the driver be dynamically unloaded

- The service control manager (SCM) is responsible for dynamically loading / unloading of drivers.

  - SCM refuses to unload a driver that does not implement **DriverUnload( )** routine thus making that driver static.

Client Application

- We propose to build a console application that would allow for dynamically loading of any .sys driver.

- The client application loads the device driver dynamically by making requests to the Service Control Manager (SCM).

- The client application would be required to pass command line arguments indicating whether we want to install (/i) or uninstall (/u) the service (driver) and the name of the service.

Building the Client

- Develop a dialog based application in VC++ using the following steps

  - Start **VC++** and Select **File | New**

  - Select **Win32 Console Application**.

  - Give **Project Name - Test** and click **OK**

  - Select **"A Hello World!" application** and click **Finish**

  - Modify generated code.

Opening Connection with SCM

- Before we can instruct the SCM to create, start, stop, or delete services we need to open a connection with it.

- The following code snippet shows how to achieve this. A complete list of the client program can be found in the *Chap02\dyndrv\Test* directory on the CD.

```
SC_HANDLE hSCM ;
hSCM = ::OpenSCManager ( NULL, NULL,
            SC_MANAGER_ALL_ACCESS ) ;
if ( hSCM == NULL)
{
    printf( "cannot open SCM" ) ;
    return ;
}
```

- The SCM provides an API function named *OpenSCManager( )* to open a connection with it.

- If due to any reason the connection could not be opened then we simply display error message reporting the error and terminate the program.

Loading the Driver

- The following code snippet shows the code snippet for loading button that dynamically loads the driver by calling SCM API functions.

```
char path[MAX_PATH] ;
::ExpandEnvironmentStrings (
  "%SystemRoot% \\\\system32\\drivers\\", path,MAX_PATH ) ;

char tmp[MAX_PATH] ;
sprintf ( tmp,"%s.sys",argv[2] ) ;
strcat ( path, tmp ) ;

SC_HANDLE hs ;
if ( stricmp(argv[1], "/i" ) == 0 )
{
    hs = ::CreateService ( hSCM, argv[2],
                argv[2],
                SERVICE_ALL_ACCESS,
                SERVICE_KERNEL_DRIVER,
                SERVICE_DEMAND_START,
                SERVICE_ERROR_NORMAL,
                path,
                NULL,
                NULL,
                NULL,
                NULL,
                NULL ) ;
    ...
}
```

- The *ExpandEnvironmentStrings( )* API function is used to figure out the absolute path of the windows system32 directory.

Loading the Driver (Cont'd)

- The *CreateService( )* API function creates a new service by dynamically creating an entry in the SCM database.

- If the *CreateService( )* function is successful then it returns a handle to the service which we have used to start the service.

- The first parameter is the handle of the SCM that we obtained earlier.

- The second parameter is the name of the service and the third is the description name of the service. For our convenience both the parameters we have passed the name of the service.

- The SCM maintains an in memory database of all the services. The *SERVICE_ALL_ACCESS* flag indicates that we want all kinds of access to the SCM database.

- The different type of access includes reading, writing, creation of services, deletion of services, locking the database etc.

Loading the Driver (Cont'd)

- The *SERVICE_KERNEL_DRIVER* parameter indicates that this service runs in kernel mode and hence is a device driver program.

- The *SERVICE_DEMAND_START* parameter marks the service as demand start so that the service is only started when we explicitly request for service start.

- The *SERVICE_ERROR_NORMAL* parameter indicates that error control should be normal. Note that these values are the same that we used in the registry script in the first chapter.

- The path parameter indicates the directory in which the .sys file resides. Note that the .sys file for the driver has to be copied in the %windir%\system32\drivers directory.

Starting the Service

- The following code snippet show the code that actually starts the execution of the service.

```
if ( ! ::StartService ( hs, 0, NULL ) )
    ReportError( ) ;
printf ( "\nsucceeded in starting the service" ) ;
CloseServiceHandle ( hs ) ;
```

- The *StartService( )* is a API function that is responsible for dynamically starting the execution of the service.

- The first parameter is the handle of the service.

- The second and the third parameter are used to pass some user defined information to the service. We have not made use of these parameters.

- Once the service has started we have closed the handle to the service using the *CloseServiceHandle( )* API function.

Unloading The Driver

- The following code snippet show how to uninstalling of the service is handled

```
if ( stricmp ( argv[1], "/u" ) == 0 )
{
    SERVICE_STATUS  status ;
    hs = OpenService ( hSCM, argv[2],
                        SERVICE_ALL_ACCESS ) ;
    if ( hs )
    {
            ControlService( hs, SERVICE_CONTROL_STOP,
                        &status ) ;
            DeleteService ( hs ) ;
            CloseServiceHandle ( hs ) ;
    }
    else
            ReportError( ) ;
}
```

- To stop the running service we have to firstly obtain the service handle by calling the *OpenService( )* API function.

- The *ControlService( )* API function helps to control (start / stop) the service us to actually stop the service.

  - We have passed the SERVICE_CONTROL_STOP parameter to

indicate that we want to stop the execution of our driver.

- The *DeleteService( )* API function removes the entry of the service from the SCM database.

Closing Connection with SCM

- Once the console application is about to end we have closed the handle of the SCM by calling the *CloseServiceHandle( )* API function.

   ::CloseServiceHandle (hSCM) ;

Testing the Driver

- Build the driver using the DDK.

- Build the client application.

- Copy the *.sys* file to the *%windir%\system32\drivers* directory.

- To load and run the driver open command prompt switch to the directory containing the client executable file and enter the following

  C:\> test /i dyndrv

- To unload the driver again enter the following command at the command prompt

  C:\> test /u dyndrv

Summary

- Code running at kernel mode cannot call any C runtime library function or API functions because these function are not designed to be callable from kernel mode

- Device Drivers make use of kernel or executive provided routines to carry out their work.

- *DbgPrint( )* routine helps to pass messages to the kernel debugger.

- Driver can be classified as static or dynamic

- Static driver remain loaded till the end of the session and require a reboot or loading / unloading

- Dynamic drivers are loaded under the control of Service Control Manager (SCM) and implement an *Unload( )* routine.

Lab 2A

Setting up a breakpoint

Write a driver that displays two messages in the *DriverEntry( )* routine. Apply a breakpoint between the two messages and watch the result on the kernel debugger.

Suggested time: 30 minutes

Answers Directory: Chap02\drvbrkpt

Files: drvbrkptg.c, makefile, sources, install.reg

Instructions:

- Create the driver program, the sources file, makefile and the registry script file as discussed in the Example\breakpt example. Make suitable changes in the sources and the registry script file.

- Build the driver using build –cZ.

- Deploy it using the registry script.

- Watch the debug activities taking place in the kernel debugger window.

Lab 2B

Driver Service Key

Write a device driver which displays the contents of the service key received by the *DriverEntry( )* routine of the device driver.

Detailed instructions are contained in the Lab 2B write-up at the end of the chapter.

Suggested time: 30 minutes

Answers Directory: Chap02\servicekey

Files: servicekey.c, makefile, sources, install.reg

Instructions:

- Create the driver program, the sources file, makefile and the registry script file as discussed in the classroom. Make suitable changes in the sources and the registry script file.

- Build the driver using **build –cZ**.

- Deploy it using the registry script.

- Test the installed driver.

Note that the service key is available at UNICODE_STRING. Convert it to an ANSI_STRING before printing it.

Chapter 3

Windows Driver Model

Windows Driver Model

Objectives

After completing this unit you will be able to:

- Understand the architectural design of an NT based OS.

- Understand how client applications can communicate with devices under NT.

- Understand how IO requests made by client applications reach Device Drivers routines.

- Write a device driver for a virtual device and a client that establishes a connection with this virtual device.

Getting Started

- Most of the operations that an application performs ultimately boils down to some kind of IO request.

- The appropriate device driver then handles these IO requests.

- This chapter focuses on how the application requests are handled by the Device Drivers. But before we begin we must understand some bit of theory involving the OS architecture.

NT OS Architecture

- To achieve portability the NT OS follows a layered architecture.

  - The three main layers are the executive, the kernel and the Hardware Abstraction Layer (HAL).

  - The following figure shows the three layers of the OS along with their components and sub components.

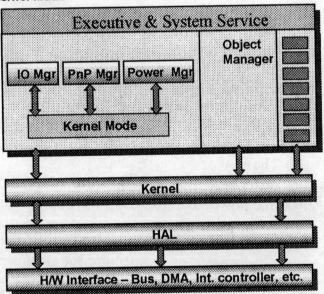

NT OS Architecture (Cont'd)

- The kernel handles the differences across different processor architectures.

  - This involves operations like interrupt and exception handling, thread synchronization, thread scheduling, context switching, multiprocessor synchronization etc.

- HAL in general manages and abstracts hardware access and device addressing in a platform independent manner.

  - HAL is responsible for communicating with the bus, direct memory access (DMA) controller, interrupt controlling etc.

  - Device Drivers are advised to use the services of the HAL to access hardware to remain portable across different processor architectures.

  - The HAL also implements features that can differ between the same processor architecture like power management, device addressing etc.

  - HAL shields the kernel from differences in the same processor architecture for example, two motherboards having different power management capabilities but based on the same processor architecture.

NT OS Architecture (Cont'd)

- The executive layer implements operations that an OS is supposed to do, which the kernel and the HAL do not implement.

  - It involves operations like process, thread management, inter process communication, memory management, networking, security and so on.

  - The executive actually refers to a specific component of the OS and does not itself implement all the entities mention above.

  - The executive works with other (executive level) components to implement all these features.

  - Collectively the executive component and other executive level component like memory manager, object manager, security manager etc are collectively often called as simply the executive.

  - The executive is one of the biggest parts of the OS.

- The Kernel and HAL together shields the rest of the OS including the executive from the difference across different processor architecture.

Dispatching Application Requests

- System Service Dispatcher is a component of the executive that is responsible for dispatching system service calls.

- System Services are functions present in the kernel mode part of the OS. System Service calls are made by issuing interrupt 2E on x86 architecture systems.

- The system service dispatcher is responsible for switching the application from user mode to kernel mode, whenever the application calls make API function whose implementation is within the kernel mode part of the OS.

The IO Subsystem

- IO Subsystem is one of the components of the executive.

- The IO subsystem itself comprises of three components

  - **IO manager** - It communicates with device drivers and also provides framework for device drivers.

  - **Plug And Play Manger** – It works closely with device drivers to implement the plug and play. The plug and play manager informs the device driver (in the form of notification packet messages) whenever a new device is found or is removed form the system.

  - **Power manager** – It implements the power management policies. The power manager notifies individual driver of the transitions in the system power state.

The Object Manager

- The Object manager happens to be one of the components of the Executive.

- Object manager is responsible for object management.

  - It handles creation, deletion, for all objects in the system.

  - The object manager also provides reference tracking which allows the system to know when an object is no longer in use so that the memory of the object can be automatically de-allocated.

  - The object manager also provides security for objects that protects objects from unauthorized access.

- Assists the IO manager in converting application request into the appropriate requests to the device drivers.

- All other components in the system make use of the services of the object manager to get work done.

  - This helps avoid unnecessary code duplication among the different components of the OS.

Object Manager's Namespace

- Device manager maintains a hierarchical tree for object management.

  - The tree contains several branches (directories) that in turn can contain further branches (directories)

  - This tree is sometimes referred to as the object manager's namespace.

  - Only a portion of the object manager's namespace is important for device driver programmers.

  - Figure 3-1 shows the object manager's namespace starting with the root branch indicated by a \. The root branch further contains Device, ?? Brach and several others as indicated by the ... box.

Object Mgr's Namespace (Cont'd)

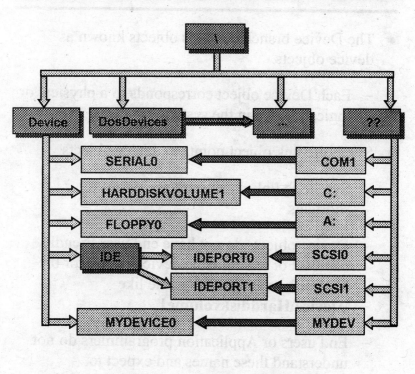

Branch   **Dev. Obj.**   **SL**

Objects Mgr's Namespace (Cont'd)

- The Device branch contains objects known as device objects.

  - Each Device object corresponds to a physical or logical device in the system.

- Symbolic link object points to device objects.

  - Symbolic link objects are analogous to shortcuts.

  - Device objects do not have end user friendly names. For example the device object for the hard disk would have a name like **\Device\Harddiskvolume1**.

  - End users or Application programmers do not understand these names and expect to communicate for example with the hard disk using symbolic link names like **C:**.

  - Symbolic link object have end user friendly names for the device objects and shoulder the responsibility of pointing to the appropriate device objects.

  - All such symbolic links are kept in a special branch whose name is **??**.

Objects Mgr's Namespace (Cont'd)

- Earlier all symbolic links used to be present in the *DosDevices* branch.

  - The **DosDevices** branch used to appear a little late in the alphabetical order.

  - **??** was invented as it can appear earlier in the list. The **DosDevices** branch is now a symbolic link to **??** Branch.

  - Only **??** Branch of the object manager's namespace is exposed to the user mode. All other branches (directories) of the object manager remain hidden from the applications running in user mode.

- The object manger resolves symbolic link names to their corresponding device object names.

  - Whenever we say **C:** in user mode, object manager looks up for **C:** symbolic link name in **??** branch and resolves it to the device object name **\Device\Harddiskvolume1**.

  - There is one unique symbolic link name for every device.

- This symbolic link name is passed to the IO manager such that it understands which device the client wants to communicate with.

- IO manager doesn't understand symbolic links. It only understands how to communicate with a device through a device object. It is the object manager that knows the mapping between symbolic link object and device object takes place.

Writing Driver For Virtual Device

- We propose to build a device driver program for a virtual (non-existing) device.

- We would name the virtual device MYDEVICE0.

  - This device name would be present in the **\Device** branch of the Object manager's namespace.

  - Here **0** represents the first instance of the device.

- We would also create a symbolic link object named *MYDEV* and make it point to *\Device\MYDEVICE0*

- A utility called *OBJDIR* in the DDK gives a list of object present in a specified branch.

Communication With Driver

- The figure shown below illustrates the detailed steps showing how the application request reaches a device driver.

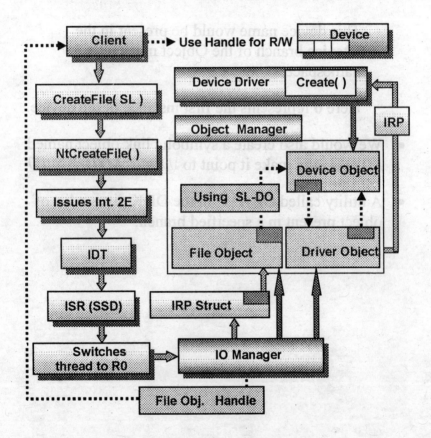

Communication With Driver
(Cont'd)

- Firstly, the Device Driver gets loaded. As soon as the Device Driver gets loaded a driver object for it is constructed by IO manger.

  - The IO manager takes the assistance of object manager to create the device object.

- IO manager calls the main entry point of the device driver i.e. *DriverEntry( )*.

  - From within the *DriveEntry( )* routine the Device Driver creates a device object and a symbolic link object.

  - The IO manager sets up pointers in the driver object and device object to point to each other.

- The client begins by calling a *CreateFile( )* API function to initiate the communication with the device.

  - The Client passes a symbolic link name to the *CreateFile( )* API function.

  - The *CreateFile( )* API function calls a undocumented function *NtCreateFile( )* which is

present in a system dynamic link library
NTDLL.DLL.

- The *NtCreateFile( )* function issues a software
interrupt **2E** to make a system service call. Due
to this a software interrupt occurs.

Communication With Driver (Cont'd)

- The processor handles the software interrupt. The processor performs a look up operation into an Interrupt Descriptor Table (IDT) to figure out the address of the Interrupt Service Routine (ISR).

- The ISR for interrupt *2E* happens to be a part of the System Service Dispatcher component of the executive.

  - The SSD switches the mode of the processor to Ring 0 on behalf of the calling thread and delegates the request to the IO manager.

- The IO manager on receiving the request creates a file object and returns a handle to the file object.

  - The IO manager takes the assistance of the object manager to convert the symbolic link name to reach the appropriate symbolic link object and then resolve it to the appropriate device object.

  - The file object's pointer is set to point to that appropriate device object.

- The IO manger builds an IRP (input/output request packet) structure to represent the client request and follows the link from file object to reach the driver object via the device object.

- The IO subsystem – IO manager, Plug and Play manager, and power manager follow a packet driver architecture in which messages and requests are described by an IRP (input/output request packet) structure.

Communication With Driver
(Cont'd)

- The driver object contains many pointers to function inside the device driver. These functions are known as dispatch routines.

- The IRP structure is then passed as a parameter to the corresponding dispatch routine.

- If the device driver successfully processes and completes the IRP request then the IO manager returns a valid handle to the file object back to the client.

  - The client subsequently uses the file handle to read and write from the target device by calling *ReadFile( )* and *WriteFile( )* API functions.

  - The IO manager simply create new messages in the form of IRP structures and keeps sending them to the appropriate dispatch routine of the device driver.

  - Once the device driver is finished with its work the client calls the *CloseHandle( )* API function that destroys the file object and the connection of the client with the Device Driver is broken.

- File object is created only once IRP structure however is created during every call.

  - Once file object is created subsequent requests are handled through the same file object.

Client For Accessing Virtual Device

- We need to build client program that communicates with the virtual device.

  - To build the client, generate **"A Hello World!"** console application in **VC++ 6.0**.

  - See **Chap03\Drv_App1\Test_DrvApp1** directory for the complete code of the client application.

Opening A Device Connection

- The code snippet shown below opens a connection with the virtual device (*MYDEVICE0*) via its symbolic link name (*MYDEV*).

```
HANDLE h = ::CreateFile ( "\\\\.\\MYDEV",
                             0, 0, NULL, OPEN_EXISTING,
                             0, NULL ) ;
if ( h == INVALID_HANDLE_VALUE )
{
    printf ( "Error opening device\n" ) ;
    return 1 ;
}
printf("sucessfully openend handle to device\n") ;
```

- *CreateFile( )* API function is used to open a connection with a device.

- The symbolic link name of the device is specified as the first parameter. The format for specifying the symbolic link name is "\\.\<symbolic link name>".

- Most of the parameters of *CreateFile( )* function remain unused. For these parameter we have passed either a *0* value or a *NULL* value.

- The *OPEN_EXISTING* is a macro that specifies that the connection is to be made with an existing device object.

Opening A Device Conn. (Cont'd)

- If the *CreateFile( )* function is successful then it returns a handle to the file object. On the other hand if the function fails then the value of the handle is *INVALID_HANDLE_VALUE*.

- The handle is collected in the variable *h*. If h is invalid then we simply print an error message and terminate the program by returning back from *main( )* with an error value of 1.

- If the handle returned is valid then we report success by displaying a message using *printf( )*.

Terminating Connection with Device

- To terminate the connection with the device the following code is used.

  CloseHandle (h) ;

- *CloseHandle( )* API function is used to terminate the connection with the device.

- The only parameter that the function requires is the handle of the file object obtained during the call to *CreateFile( )*.

- *CloseHandle( )* function cleans up any resources that were allocated during the call to *CreateFile( )*.

- The file object created during a call to *CreateFile( )* is deleted.

Driver For Virtual Device

- We would now discuss the code of the driver for the virtual device.

  - See **Chap03\Drv_App1** directory for the complete listing of the driver code.

Extending Device Object Structure

- The code snippet shown below defines a structure that helps us to dynamically extend the device object structure.

```
struct DEVICE_EXTENSION
{
    UNICODE_STRING SymLinkName ;
} ;
```

// More code

- Device Extension is a IO manager provided feature for extending the device object structure.

  - Device object is a standard (fixed length) structure.

  - We wish to extend it to also have additional information (a symbolic link name basically as a UNICODE string) in it.

  - There is a provision to extent the structure while creating the device object programmatically. The structure helps us to keep additional information in a device object and hence is said to extend the device object.

Driver For Virtual Device (Cont'd)

- A UNICODE string containing the symbolic link name is kept in the device extension structure

  - This is necessary because symbolic link object that we would soon construct would have to be later on freed. The object manager service for freeing the symbolic link object would require us to pass the symbolic link name.

  - To preserve the symbolic link name we have kept the string in the device extension structure.

The DriverEntry( ) Routine

- The *DriverEntry( )* routine for this driver is supposed to do the following

  - Register dispatch routines for **IRP_MJ_CREATE** and **IRP_MJ_CLOSE** requests.

  - Create device object named **"MyDevice0"**.

  - Create a symbolic link to **"MyDevice0"** named **"MYDEV"**.

Registering Dispatch Routines

- Code snippet shown below registers dispatch routines for *IRP_MJ_CREATE* and *IRP_MJ_CLOSE* requests.

```
extern "C"
NTSTATUS DriverEntry ( PDRIVER_OBJECT pDrvObj,
                       PUNICODE_STRING pRegPath )
{
    // code to register Unload routine
    pDrvObj->MajorFunction[IRP_MJ_CREATE] = Create ;
    pDrvObj->MajorFunction[IRP_MJ_CLOSE] = Close ;
    // more code
}
```

- The Driver Object contains an array of pointers called MajorFunction.

  - Each Dispatch routine has the same signature hence an array of function pointers is used.

  - The **MajorFunction** array of function pointers keeps track of all the dispatch routines for a driver.

  - We have only registered two of the dispatch functions of them.

  - The **IRP_MJ_CREATE** and **IRP_MJ_CLOSE** are macros that expand to some numeric value to refer to a specific pointer of the array.

- The word **MJ** in IRP macro refers to major function

Reg. Dispatch Routines (Cont'd)

- When the client calls the *CreateFile( )* API function the IO manager builds a IRP packet with the code of *IRP_MJ_CREATE.*

- The IO manager then looks up in the Major function array to find the name of the dispatch routine that handles the request.

- Using a pointer to a function the IO manager calls the dispatch routine.

- When we don't register dispatch routine they are set up to point to a routine within the IO manager that simply fails the requests.

- IRP macros are called IO Function Codes in DD terminology.

Creating Device Object

- The code snippet shown below creates a device
  object named "MyDevice0" in the object manager's
  namespace.

```
UNICODE_STRING devname ;
RtlInitUnicodeString ( &devname, L\\Device\\MyDevice0 ) ;
PDEVICE_OBJECT pDevObj ;
NTSTATUS s ;
s=IoCreateDevice ( pDrvObj,
                   sizeof ( DEVICE_EXTENSION ), &devname,
                   FILE_DEVICE_UNKNOWN,
                   0,
                   TRUE,
                   &pDevObj ) ;

if ( ! NT_SUCCESS ( s ) )
    return s ;
```

Creating Device Object (Cont'd)

- *RtlInitUnicodeString( )* is a kernel mode runtime routine that device driver calls to initialize a UNICODE string variable.

  - This function is used to initialize the string containing the complete path of the device object name **\Device\MyDevice0.**

  - **0** indicates the instance number of the device.

  - A machine having two parallel ports would still have a common driver for both of these ports. Since **1** parallel port driver is serving **2** parallel ports the driver would construct **2** device objects with symbolic like **LPT1** and **LPT2.** This is convention, not a rule.

- *IoCreateDevice( )* is an IO Manager service for creating Device object.

  - The first parameter is the pointer to driver object. This is necessary since the driver object maintains a linked list of all the device objects created by it.

  - The second parameter is the extra number of bytes that needs to be allocated for dynamically

extending the device object. We have passed the
size of our device extension structure.

Creating Device Object (Cont'd)

- The third parameter is a Unicode string specifying the name of the device object.

- The fourth parameter is a macro that specifies the type of the physical device (display, storage etc) that the device object refers to. Since, our device is virtual we have specified the device type as unknown.

- The fifth parameter indicates the nature of device like read only device, removable device etc. For custom category device we are required to use a 0 value.

- The sixth parameter (**TRUE**) specifies that an exclusive access from the client is required i.e- if we call *CreateFile( )* twice or if two clients use *CreateFile( )*, the second call would fail.

- More complicated drivers would have a value **FALSE** and accordingly handle the request by queuing it.

- The last parameter is the address of a device object structure that is set on successful completion by the service.

Creating Symbolic Link Object

- The code snippet shown below creates a symbolic link object named "MYDEV" to the device object created earlier.

```
DEVICE_EXTENSION* pDevExt =
( DEVICE_EXTENSION* ) pDevObj->DeviceExtension ;

UNICODE_STRING  linkname ;
RtlInitUnicodeString ( &linkname, L"\\??\\MYDEV" ) ;
pDevExt -> SymLinkName = linkname ;
s = IoCreateSymbolicLink ( &linkname, &devname ) ;
if ( !NT_SUCCESS ( s ) )
{
    IoDeleteDevice ( pDevObj ) ;
    return s ;
}
DbgPrint ( "In driver entry\n" ) ;
return STATUS_SUCCESS ;
```

- The pointer to the device extension structure is available from the device object.

- A UNICODE string variable is initialized to hold the name of the symbolic link object.

- A UNICODE string specifying the symbolic link name for our device object is initialized and a copy of it is stored in the device extension structure.

- The *IoCreateSymbolicLink( )* service creates the actual symbolic link object.

Creating Sym. Link Object (Cont'd)

- The *IoCreateService( )* requires the name of the device object so that it can initialize the newly created symbolic link object to correctly refer to the appropriate device object.

- If the creation of the symbolic link object fails then we have deleted the device object and returned the failure code from the *DriverEntry( )* routine thus, unloading the driver from memory.

Unloading The Driver

- The code for handling the unload event is shown below.

```
void Unload ( PDRIVER_OBJECT pDrvObj )
{
    PDEVICE_OBJECT pDevObj = pDrvObj -> DeviceObject ;
    DEVICE_EXTENSION* pe = ( DEVICE_EXTENSION *)
                        pe -> DeviceExtension ;

    IoDeleteSymbolicLink ( &pe-> SymLinkName ) ;
    IoDeleteDevice ( pDrvObj->DeviceObject ) ;
    DbgPrint ( "In driver unload\n" ) ;
}
```

- The *Unload( )* routine is implemented to make the driver dynamic.

- We need to free up any resources that we might have allocated.

  - We begin by obtaining a device extension pointer from the device object and deleting the symbolic link object by specifying its name.

  - We also then delete the device object. The pointer to the device object is available from the driver object.

Object Relationships

- The figure shown in the slide would help in understanding the relationship between the various objects.

- The driver object contains a pointer to the device object.

- The device object also in turn keeps a pointer to its owner the driver object.

- The device object contains a pointer to the device extension structure.

- The device extension contains a member of type UNICODE_STRING that keeps the symbolic link name.

Handling Create Request

- When the client calls *CreateFile( )* API function to establish a connection with the device the IO manager generates *IRP_MJ_CREATE* message.

- The code for handling the *IRP_MJ_CREATE* request is shown below.

```
NTSTATUS Create( PDEVICE_OBJECT pDevObj, PIRP plrp )
{
    plrp -> IoStatus.Status = STATUS_SUCCESS ;
    plrp -> IoStatus.Information = 0 ;
    IoCompleteRequest ( plrp, IO_NO_INCREMENT ) ;
    DbgPrint ( "In Create\n" ) ;
    return STATUS_SUCCESS ;
}
```

- The Create function was registered in the *DriverEntry( )* routine as dispatch routine for the *IRP_MJ_CREATE* message.

- Implementing the *Create( )* dispatch routine and successfully completing the IRP request is mandatory otherwise the *CreateFile( )* API function made by the client would simply fail.

- To complete a IRP request IoManager provides a service called *IoCompleteRequest( )*.

- The IRP structure contains a nested structure called **IoStatus** that is used to specify the completion status (success / failure) of the IRP request.

Handling Create Request (Cont'd)

- The **IoStatus** structure also has a member called **Information** that indicates the number of bytes successfully transferred during the request.

- Completing the request is not as simple as simply returning from this function.

  - The application thread stands blocked when IO request was made through an API function.

  - Moreover the results in IRP have to be copied from system address space (upper 2 GB) to user address space (lower 2 GB) before the app thread resumes the blocked state.

  - This routine does the copying and then the application thread resumes.

  - There are several such activities that need to be performed hence we need to call the IO manager service to complete the IO request.

- The *IoCompleteRequest( )* service has an extra parameter that helps to temporarily increase (boost) the priority of the calling thread

- This boost compensates for the time the thread was blocked during the processing of the request.

- We are not requesting priority boost (**IO_NO_INCREMENT**) since we have not consumed any time in completing the IO request.

Handling Create Request (Cont'd)

- In real life boosting would be necessary, (especially when heavily layered drivers work for a device) to compensate for the time the application thread was blocked during the IO request.

- If we return a *STATUS_SUCCESS* value the IO manager in turn returns handle to file object back to the client.

- If we fail to return proper status from *Create()* IO manager in turn would return INVALID_HANDLE_VALUE to the client.

Handling the Close Request

- When the client calls *CloseHandle( )* API function to terminate the connection with the device the IO manager generates IRP_MJ_CLOSE message.

- The code for handling the IRP_MJ_CLOSE request is shown below.

```
NTSTATUS Close ( PDEVICE_OBJECT pDevObj, PIRP pIrp )
{
    pIrp -> IoStatus.Status = STATUS_SUCCESS ;
    pIrp -> IoStatus.Information = 0 ;
    IoCompleteRequest ( pIrp, IO_NO_INCREMENT ) ;
    DbgPrint ( "In close\n" ) ;
    return STATUS_SUCCESS ;
}
```

- The *Close( )* function was registered from *DriverEntry( )* as a dispatch routine (handler) for the *IRP_MJ_CLOSE* message.

- Implementing this dispatch routine is necessary otherwise the *CloseHandle( )* API function that the client would later on call would fail.

- The *Close( )* dispatch routine is ideally supposed to clean up any resources. We have not allocated any resources so what remains is completing the IRP packet with success.

- The code for completing the IRP with success is the same as that of *Create( )*.

Testing The Driver

- To test the driver carry out the following steps

  - Build the driver.

  - Copy the **.sys** file to the
    %windir%\system32\drivers directory.

  - Load the driver using the generic **.sys** loader
    program that we created earlier.

  - Build & execute the client application.

- As soon as the client application is run the success
  message should appear in the console window.

Summary

- System services are functions present within the kernel mode part of the OS. To make a system service call on an x86 system interrupt 2Eh is issued.

- System service dispatcher is an executive component that is responsible for dispatching the system service calls to appropriate component of the OS.

- Application requests are internally represented by IO Request Packet (IRP) structures. The handler function for the IRP requests are known as dispatch routines.

- Client applications make use of *CreateFile( )* API function to open a connection with devices and *CloseHandle( )* API function to terminate the connection.

- The three objects that play a key role in communicating application requests to device drivers are file object, device object and driver object.

- Object Manager is a component of the executive and is responsible for management of objects and assists the IO manager to resolve symbolic link names to their corresponding device object names.

- The IO system is a component of the executive and it comprises of 3 components IO manager, Plug and Play manager and Power Manager.

Lab 3A

Viewing The Object Manager Namespace

Using the objdir utility watch the contents of various branches of the object manager's namespace.

Suggested time: 15 minutes

Instructions:

- Open the checked build environment from the start menu

- Issue the following commands from the command prompt to view the contents of the different branches of the object manager's namespace

  objdir \?? – displays the contents of all symbolic link objects
  objdir \Devices – displays the contents of the device branch.

Lab 3B

The Device Object Structure

Write a device driver that displays the following elements of the device object structure:

DriverObject – contains the address of the driver object structure

DeviceExtension – contains the address of the device extension structure.

Suggested time: 30 minutes

Answers Directory: Chap03\devobj

Files: devobj.c, makefile, sources, install.reg

Instructions:

- Create the driver program, the source file and the makefile.

- Build the driver and deploy it using a registry script. Test the installed driver.

- Check out the debug messages in the kernel debugger window.

Chapter 4

Communication Between Application And Device Driver

Communication Between

Application & Device Driver

Objectives

After completing this unit you will be able to:

- Understand the memory management model of NT.

- Understand how client applications can actually read/ write from/to devices under NT.

- Write a device driver for a virtual loop back device and a client that reads/writes from/to this virtual loop back device.

Getting Started

- Before we begin writing the driver and the client application we need to understand the memory management model used by NT_OS.

- We begin by understanding the following concepts

  - Virtual Memory

  - System address space and user address space.

  - Demand paged virtual memory.

  - Address translation.

Memory Management

- Computer systems never seem to have enough memory, no matter how much memory is installed.

  - As the complexity of software programs increases applications tend to become more memory hungry.

  - The need for running more applications simultaneously increases memory requirements.

- One of the most complex and difficult tasks faced by OS is managing the limited physical memory present on a computer.

  - The OS must divide physical memory among many processes that might be running simultaneously, giving each process an appropriate memory share.

  - Over the years many strategies have been developed to overcome this limitation and the most successful of these is the virtual memory.

Virtual Memory

- Each running process is provided with the illusion that a computer has more memory than that is actually present.

  - The mechanism that implements this illusion is known as virtual memory.

  - The Memory Manager (or Virtual Memory Manager VMM) is one of the sub components of the executive subsystem in NT that is responsible for implementing NT's virtual memory management.

- Processes access memory through their virtual memory address space.

  - Virtual memory address space is simply a range of all the possible virtual memory addresses.

  - The size of a process' virtual address space is 4GB. This is because NT works in 32-bit environment and hence a pointer that stores an address can be of maximum 32-bit.

  - Thus, a process can theoretically allocate 4GB of code and data. However, most computers today have comparatively very less physical memory (in Megabytes).

- The 4GB address space of a process is therefore known as virtual memory, because it doesn't directly correspond to physical memory.

Address Space Layout

- The 4GB address space is divided into two equal halves one for the private use of the process and the other half for the OS usage.

- Figure shows the layout of the address space for a process.

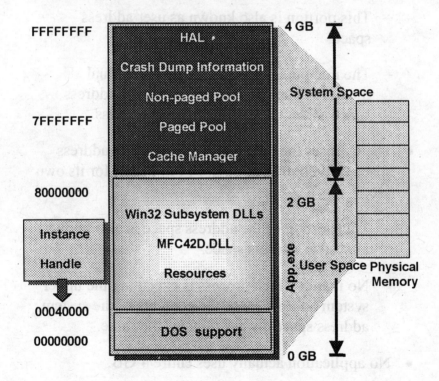

Address Space Layout (Cont'd)

- An address space is simply a range of all possible address.

- Processes use the lower half of the total 4-GB virtual address space (0x00000000 through 0x7FFFFFFF) for their unique private storage.

  - This portion is also known as user address space.

  - The mappings of the lower half of virtual memory change to reflect the virtual address space of the currently executing process.

- The OS uses the upper half (2GB) of the address space (80000000h through FFFFFFFFh) for its own use.

  - This portion of the address space is also known as system address space.

  - No matter which process is executing the upper system address space the contents of the system address space always remains the same.

- No application actually uses entire 4 GB.

- The actual used portion within the 4GB address space is mapped into a much smaller physical space.

Translating Virtual Address

- The memory management unit (MMU) present inside the processor manages physical and virtual memory in blocks called pages.

  - On x86 processors, the size of a page is 4KB.

  - A computer's physical memory pages are known as page frames, which the processor numbers consecutively with page frame numbers (PFNs).

- When a process references its virtual memory, it does so with a 32-bit pointer, and the MMU's job is to determine the corresponding location in the physical memory to which the virtual address maps.

  - The MMU determines this location by dividing the 32-bit pointer address into three separate indexes, page directory index, page table index, and page byte offset.

  - The MMU uses each index in a three-step address translation process as illustrated in the figure shown below.

Translating Virtual Address (Cont'd)

- The MMU locates a table known as the page directory in the physical memory.

  - A special processor register known as page directory register contains the address of the page directory table.

  - On x86-based processors the page directory register is called Control Register 3 (CR3).

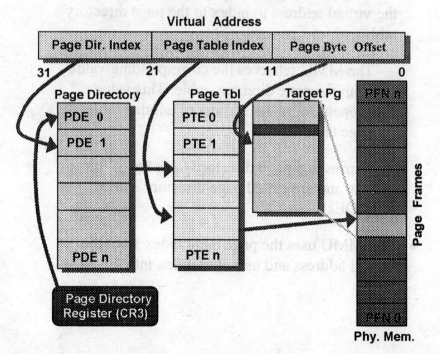

Translating Virtual Address (Cont'd)

- Each process has its own private page directory, and the address of that directory is stored in the process' control block (PCB) data structure.

  - Whenever the thread scheduler switches from one process to another, it updates the page directory register with the value stored in the control block of the process that takes over the CPU.

- Next the MMU uses the page directory index from the virtual address to index to the page directory table.

  - The MMU retrieves the corresponding value from the page directory table. This value happens to be the address of another table, the page table.

  - Entries in a page directory table are 32 bits in size and are called page directory entries (PDEs).

- The MMU uses the page table index from the virtual address and uses it to index into the page table.

- The entry the MMU finds at the page table index identifies a page frame in physical memory.

- Entries in a page table are 32-bits in size and are called page table entries (PTEs).

• Finally, the MMU uses the page byte offset as an index into the physical page to reach the data that the process wants to reference.

Demand Based Virtual Memory

- When a process gets launched it is told by memory manager that 4 GB is allocated to it without really allocating it.

- As and when the application tries to use portions of its 4 GB address space a memory fault occurs.

  - Memory Manager handles the fault.

  - Fault handler allocates a few pages of physical memory to satisfy the request.

  - The instruction responsible for fault is re-executed by moving the EIP pointer back.

  - This mechanism is known as demand based memory because memory is allocated only on demand when it is actually needed for use.

Paging

- Most systems have much less physical memory than the total virtual memory in use by the running processes.

- To free physical memory the memory manages writes, or pages out, some of the memory contents to disk.

  - Paging out data to disk frees physical memory so that it can be used for other processes or for the OS itself.

  - When a thread accesses a virtual address that has been paged out to disk, the virtual memory manager loads the information back into memory from disk.

  - Hardware support enables the memory manager to page without the knowledge or assistance of processes or threads.

  - Application need not be modified in any way to take advantage of Paging.

- Some of the critical Kernel Mode routines expect that the memory they access should not be paged.

- Critical routines like Interrupt Service Routines and Deferred Procedure calls can only access non-paged memory.

- Accessing paged memory results in a crash (blue screen of death).

Reading & Writing From Devices

- We now try to develop a driver for a virtual loop back device.

  - The device driver would not talk to any physical hardware hence the name virtual.

  - Loop Back indicates that the device driver would store the information send to it in the write request and return back the same information unchanged back to the client for a read request.

- The working of the virtual loop back device is shown in the following figure

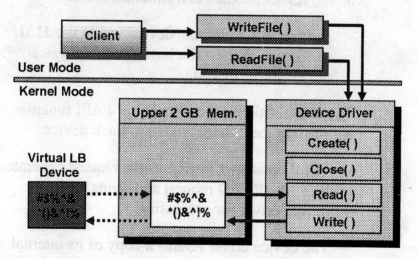

Reading & Writing From Devices (Cont'd)

- A client uses *WriteFile( )* API functions to write to the virtual loop back device.

  – The write requests is interpreted by the IO manager that translates it IRP_MJ_WRITE request.

  – The IRP_MJ_WRITE request is handled by the **Write( )** dispatch routines of the device driver.

- The *Write( )* dispatch routine present in the device driver copies the data in its internal buffer.

  – A driver for a physical device would use HAL services to transfer the buffer to the physical device for processing.

- The client makes use of *ReadFile( )* API function for reading form the virtual loop back device.

  – The IO manager intercepts the request generates IRP_MJ_READ request and sends it to the device driver for processing.

  – The device driver returns a copy of its internal buffer back to the client.

Buffered I/O Technique

- There are many techniques that a device driver can use to handle read and write requests from client application.

  - The difference between the various techniques is the way device driver accesses the application programs buffer (data).

- Here we would see how writing and reading takes place when Buffered I/O technique is used.

  - The following figure shows the working of the buffered I/O Technique.

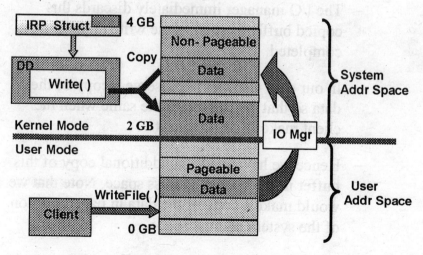

Buffered I/O Technique (Cont'd)

- When the client issues a *WriteFile( )* API request the I/O manager copies the buffer specified in the request to a non-pagable area of the system address space.

    – The IO manager then creates a IRP structure IRP_MJ_WRITE and passes it to the device driver.

    – One of the members of the IRP structure contains a pointer to the starting address of the copied data in the system address space.

    – The I/O manager immediately discards this copied buffer as soon as the write request is completed.

    – In our case we want to preserve a copy of the data so that we can return the same when the client makes a read request.

    – Hence we have made an additional copy of this buffer in the system address space. Note that we would make a copy of the data in paged portion of the system address space.

- The reading procedure for the buffered I/O technique will be as per the following steps.

- The client calls *ReadFile( )* API function and specifies a empty buffer.

- The IO manager builds IRP_MJ_READ function to represent the request and allocates a buffer in the system address space.

Buffered I/O Technique (Cont'd)

- The device driver receives the request and copies the earlier copied data to the IO manager's allocated buffer.

- When the device driver completes the request the IO manager copies the system address space back to the user mode buffer

- Finally the client receives the data in its buffer

- This technique is known as buffered technique since a extra copy of the user buffer is made in the system address space.

Layered Driver Model

- WDM (Windows Driver Model) Drivers for NT OS follow what is know as a layered Model.

- Drivers for complex device are split into multiple drivers.

  - These device drivers form a vertical stack as shown in the following figure.

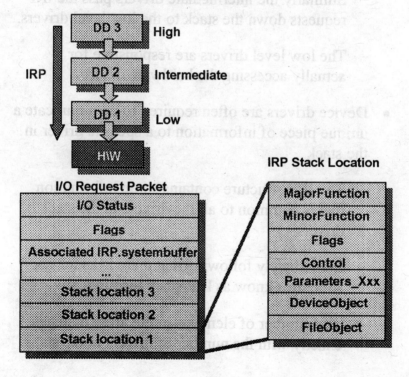

Layered Driver Model (Cont'd)

- – The top of the stack consists of high-level driver that accepts IRP for client requests.

- – The high level driver do whatever processing is required and if necessary pass the IRP requests to intermediate drivers.

- – Similarly the intermediate drivers pass the IRP requests down the stack to the low level drivers.

- – The low level drivers are responsible for actually accessing the hardware device.

- Device drivers are often required to communicate a unique piece of information to a specific driver in the stack.

  - – The IRP structure contains some information that is common to all the drivers in the stack of drivers.

  - – Immediately following that there is an array of structures know as IRP stack location.

  - – The number of elements in the array matches exactly with the number of drivers in the stack.

- The IRP that flows though a 3 layered driver stack would contain three stack locations as a part of the IRP structure.

- Each IRP stack location contains information specific to a particular driver in the driver stack.

- Figure shows the details of the IRP stack location structure. Note that for a one layered driver stack only one stack location would be present inside the IRP structure

Layered Driver Model (Cont'd)

- Device Driver can only access its own stack location or the stack location of the driver below it.

    - This is because a driver always sends information down the stack so it would only be required to change the stack location of the driver below it and not above it.

Virtual Loop Back Driver Client

- The code snippet for reading writing form the virtual loop back driver is shown below.

- For a complete listing of the code see *Chap04\readwrite\Test_ReadWrite* directory on the CD.

- Firstly the client calls the *CreateFile( )* API function to establish a connection with the virtual loop back device using its symbolic link name.

- Then the client makes use of *WriteFile( )* and *ReadFile( )* API function to write and read form the device

- Lastly the client closes the connection using the *CloseHandle( )* API function.

Opening Connection with LB Device

- The code snippet shows how the client establishes connection with the loop back device.

```
# include "stdafx.h"
# include <windows.h>

void main( )
{
     HANDLE  h = ::CreateFile ( "\\\\.\\mydev",
                     GENERIC_READ | GENERIC_WRITE,
                     0, NULL, OPEN_EXISTING,
                     FILE_ATTRIBUTE_NORMAL, NULL ) ;

     // more code
}
```

- Note that the client uses GENERIC_READ and GENERIC_WRITE macros in the *CreateFile( )* function.

- These flags are necessary otherwise the call to *ReadFile( )* and *WriteFile( )* API functions would simply fail.

Writing Data to LB Device

- Following code shows how the client manages to writes data to the virtual loop back device.

```
char  Buff1[ ] = "This is a test" ;
DWORD  bw ;
BOOL  status ;
status = ::WriteFile ( h, Buff1, sizeof ( Buff1 ), &bw, NULL ) ;
if ( !status )
{
    printf ( "WriteFile failed\n" ) ;
    return ;
}
```

- The client makes use of *WriteFile( )* API function to write to the device.

  - The *WriteFile( )* API function requires the handle of file object obtained during the call to *CreateFile( )*.

  - The second parameter is the address of the buffer to be written and the third parameter is the size of the buffer

  - The fourth parameter is the address of a variable that would be set with the count of bytes that the function was successfully able to write.

  - The fifth parameter is not used.

- The function returns a nonzero value if it is successful.

Reading Data From VLB Device

- Reading from the device is similar to write except that the client would now make a call to the *ReadFile()* API function.

```
char Buff2 [ 80 ] ;
DWORD br ;
status = ::ReadFile ( h, Buff2, sizeof ( Buff2 ), &br, NULL ) ;
if ( ! status )
{
    printf ( " ReadFile Failed " ) ;
    return ;
}
```

- The parameters of the *ReadFile( )* API function are similar to that of the *WriteFile( )* function.

- The fourth parameter returns the actual number of bytes that the function was successfully able to read.

Writing The VLB Driver

- We now discuss the driver code for the virtual loop back device.

- Note that we would be discussing the code that has changed from the previous program. The complete source code for the VLB driver can be found in the *Chap04\readwrite* directory on the CD.

```
struct DEV_EXT
{
    UNICODE_STRING SymLink ;
    void* pBuff ;
    ULONG BuffSize ;
};
```

- The device extension structure for this driver includes two new additional members.

    - A void pointer **pBuff** that would hold the data send by the client

    - A unsigned long variable **BuffSize** that would keep track of the length of the buffer.

DriverEntry( ) Routine

- The code snippet for the *DriverEntry( )* routine registers is shown below.

```
extern "C"
NTSTATUS DriverEntry ( PDRIVER_OBJECT pDrvObj,
                          PUNICODE_STRING pRegPath )
{
    pDrvObj->DriverUnload = Unload ;
    pDrvObj->MajorFunction[IRP_MJ_CREATE] = Create ;
    pDrvObj->MajorFunction[IRP_MJ_CLOSE] = Close ;
    pDrvObj->MajorFunction[IRP_MJ_READ] = Read ;
    pDrvObj->MajorFunction[IRP_MJ_WRITE] = Write ;

    // code to create device object
    pDevObj -> Flags |= DO_BUFFERED_IO ;

    DEV_EXT *pe ;
    pe =( DEV_EXT * ) pDevObj->DeviceExtension ;
    pe-> pBuff = NULL ;
    pe-> BuffSize = 0 ;
    // more code.
    return STATUS_SUCCESS ;
}
```

- The *DriverEntry( )* routine begins by registering the entry points of the device driver.

    - The four dispatch routines are registered by filling in the array of pointers named **MajorFunction**.

- Note that we have registered the dispatch routines for handling the **IRP_MJ_WRITE** and **IRP_MJ_READ** requests.

DriverEntry( ) Routine (Cont'd)

- The buffered IO technique for transferring data between the client and the device driver is specified.

  - The flags member of the device object structure is bitwise ored with **DO_BUFFERED_IO**.

  - Bitwise Oring is necessary so that the existing characteristics of the device object would not be lost.

- The initial state of the internal buffer is empty hence *pBuff* and *BuffSize* variables are set to *NULL* and *0*.

Write Dispatch Routine

- The code for the write dispatch routine is shown below.

```
NTSTATUS Write ( PDEVICE_OBJECT pDevObj, PIRP pIrp)
{
    DEV_EXT* pe ;
    pe = ( DEV_EXT* ) pDevObj -> DeviceExtension ;
    if ( pe -> pBuff != NULL )
    {
        ExFreePool ( pe -> pBuff ) ;
        pe -> pBuff = NULL ;
        pe -> BuffSize = 0 ;

    }
    PIO_STACK_LOCATION pLoc ;
    pLoc = IoGetCurrentIrpStackLocation ( pIrp ) ;
    ULONG xferSize = pLoc->parameters.Write.Length ;
    pe -> pBuff = ExAllocatePool ( PagedPool, xferSize ) ;
    if ( pe -> pBuff == NULL )
    {
        status = STATUS_INSUFFICIENT_RESOURCES ;
        xferSize = 0 ;

    }
    else
    {
        void*  userBuff = pIrp->AssociatedIrp.SystemBuffer ;
        pe -> BuffSize = xferSize ;
        RtlCopyMemory ( pe -> pBuff, userBuff, xferSize ) ;
    }
    pIrp->IoStatus.Status = STATUS_SUCCESS ;
    pIrp->IoStatus.Information = xferSize ;
    IoCompleteRequest ( pIrp, IO_NO_INCREMENT ) ;
```

```
        return status ;
    }
```

Write Dispatch Routine (Cont'd)

- The Write dispatch routine is called in response to the IRP_MJ_WRITE message sent by the I/O manager.

  - The I/O manager sends this message when the client calls the *WriteFile( )* function to write information to a device.

  - By the time the execution control reaches the Write dispatch routine the IO manager would have finished copying of buffer from user address space to non-paged area of the system address space.

  - In the write dispatch routine we intend to copy the buffer the system address space to our own buffer.

- To handle the write request the following steps are followed.

  - Obtain a pointer to the IO manager copied buffer and the size of the buffer

  - Check if the internal buffer is non-empty and if it is de-allocate the memory. This is necessary if the client calls *WriteFile( )* again before closing the handle to avoid any memory leaks.

- Allocate paged memory of the same size as that of the client supplied buffer.

- Copy the contents of IO manager buffer to the allocated memory.

- Complete the **IRP_MJ_WRITE** request specifying the number of bytes successfully written to the device.

Write Dispatch Routine (Cont'd)

- The following functions and structures are required to carry out the above mentioned operations.

  - The starting address of the IO manager copied buffer is available in the stack location structure of our driver.

  - The stack location structure for the current driver can be obtained by calling the IO manager service *IoGetCurrentIrpStackLocation( )*.

  - The byte length of the client supplied buffer is available in an nested structure called **Write**.

  - The *ExAllocatePool( )* service of the executive is used to allocate memory.

  - The first parameter of the service indicates what type of memory (paged / non-paged) has to be allocated. The second parameter of the service indicates the number of bytes to allocate.

  - The *ExAllocatePool( )* return the starting address of the newly allocated memory. If the *ExAllocatePool( )* service fails it returns NULL.

Dispatch Routine (Cont'd)

- Copying of memory is achieved using the kernel mode runtime library function *RtlCopyMemory( )*.

  - The first parameter is the address of the target buffer

  - The second parameter is the address of the source buffer.

  - The third parameter indicates the number of bytes to be copied.

Read Dispatch Routine

- The read dispatch routine is mostly similar to the write dispatch routine.

- The code for the read dispatch routine is shown below.

```
NTSTATUS Read ( PDEVICE_OBJECT pDevObj,PIRP pIrp )
{
    DEV_EXT* pe ;
    pe = ( DEV_EXT* ) pDevObj-> DeviceExtension ;
    PIO_STACK_LOCATION  pLoc ;
    pLoc = IoGetCurrentIrpStackLocation ( pIrp ) ;
    ULONG xferSize = pLoc->Parameters.Read.Length ;
    xferSize = ( xferSize < pe -> Size ) ? xferSize
                                         : pe -> size ;
    PVOID userBuff = pIrp -> AssociatedIrp.SystemBuffer ;
    RtlCopyMemory ( userBuff,pe->pBuff, xferSize ) ;
    pIrp->IoStatus.Status = STATUS_SUCCESS;
    pIrp->IoStatus.Information = xferSize ;
    IoCompleteRequest ( pIrp, IO_NO_INCREMENT ) ;
    return status ;
}
```

- The following difference can be noted

  - The internal buffer is copied to the IO mangers buffer.

  - The read dispatch routine checks whether the request number of bytes for the read operation exceeds the size of the previously written buffer and accordingly adjusts the transfer size.

Close Dispatch Routine

- When the client calls the *CloseHandle( )* function the close dispatch routine gets called.

- We need to de-allocate the memory if any and complete the request.

- The code snippet for the close dispatch routine is shown below.

```
NTSTATUS Close(PDEVICE_OBJECT pDevObj, PIRP pIrp)
{
    DEV_EXT* pe ;
    pe=DEV_EXT * ) pDevObj -> DeviceExtension ;
    if ( pe -> pBuff != NULL )
    {
        ExFreePool ( pe -> pBuff ) ;
        pe -> pBuff = NULL ;
        pe -> BuffSize = 0 ;
    }
    pIrp -> IoStatus.Status = STATUS_SUCCESS ;
    pIrp -> IoStatus.Information = 0 ;
    IoCompleteRequest ( pIrp, IO_NO_INCREMENT ) ;
    return STATUS_SUCCESS ;
}
```

- To reach the address of the buffer we have firstly obtained a pointer to the device extension structure from the device object.

Close Dispatch Routine (Cont'd)

- The OS does not free the memory automatically.

  - The OS automatically frees up any resource like memory open handles for a application program only whenever the program terminates.

  - The OS however does not provide this facility for kernel mode code.

  - If we do not free up any memory and simply allow the driver to unload then it would create a memory leak that would remain for the entire session of windows.

Summary

- NT provides a 4GB address space for each running application.

- The upper 2GB of address space is known as system address space and contains the code and data of operating system and device drivers.

- The lower 2GB of address space is used for holding the code and data of the application that is active.

- Under low memory conditions the OS pages out data to disk. When required the paged memory is read back from the disk.

- The client application makes use of *ReadFile( )* and *WriteFile( )* API functions to read and write from a device.

- The device driver handles the request by implementing dispatch routines for the IRP_MJ_READ and IRP_MJ_WRITE requests.

- Buffered IO techniques allows the client and device driver to easily exchange memory buffers.

Lab 4

Driver For Virtual Device

Write a device driver program that accepts a string from the client application and converts it to uppercase. The new string should be returned back to the client.

Suggested time: 60 minutes

Answers Directory: Chap04\uppercase

Files: uppercase.cpp, sources, makefile, install.reg

Instructions:

- Use the readwrite example as a base for creating the driver program, the sources file and the makefile.

- Modify the *Write( )* dispatch routine so as to convert the client supplied buffer to uppercase.

- Build and deploy the driver

- Run the client application located in **Chap04\readwrite\test** on the CD and verify that the string send by the client actually gets converted to uppercase.

Chapter 5

Hardware Basics

Hardware Basics

Objectives

After completing this unit you will be able to:

- Understand the basics of hardware environment.

- Understand how device interrupt mechanisms works.

- Understand different data transfer mechanisms used by devices.

Getting Started

- Most of the drivers that we have written so far did not interact with any physical device. A real world driver however mostly interacts with a physical device.

- We propose to develop such a real world driver that interacts with a physical device.

- Before we actually begin to develop this driver we need to understand the general concepts and mechanisms for working with any hardware device.

- These general concepts involve understanding the following

  - Connection of devices to the CPU (microprocessor) via the bus.

  - Device registers used for communication between the device and the CPU.

  - Device register's mapping to CPU address space.

  - Hardware interrupts - a mechanism for the device to inform the system software about critical events.

- Interrupt handling under NT OS.

- Software and hardware interrupt levels – IRQLs.

- Different mechanisms that devices follow to transfer data between themselves and the CPU.

Connection With Devices

- All the devices (external or internal) get connected to the CPU via a set of parallel lines called bus.

  - CPU and devices communicate through a bus.

  - The bus helps the CPU to physically get connected to the device (more correctly device registers).

  - Device registers are locations within the device that can be read / written.

- All the chips present on the motherboard are connected to the CPU in a parallel fashion as shown in the figure.

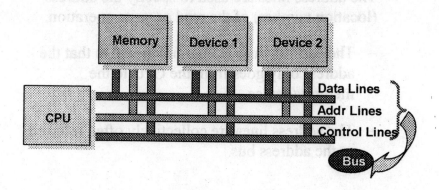

Connection With Devices (Cont'd)

- The bus further consists of data lines, address lines, and control lines.

- Data lines are solely used only for transferring data.

  - During a read operation the data flows from the device or memory to the CPU.

  - During a write operation the data flows from the CPU to the device/memory.

  - The data lines are often collectively referred to as the data bus.

  - The data bus is bi-directional.

- The address lines are used to specify the address (location number) of the read or write operation.

  - The address lines are unidirectional in that the address only goes from the CPU to the memory/device.

  - The address lines are collectively often referred as the address bus.

- The control lines are additional lines that are used for communication between the CPU and the target device/memory.

  - For example, one of the control lines is used to indicate whether the address on the address bus is memory mapped or port mapped address.

  - Another line indicates whether the operation is read/ write.

Connection With Devices (Cont'd)

- The width of the bus is particularly important since it has a direct implication on the amount of information that can travel at a time over it.

  - A system with a 16-bit data bus will require 2 trips for transferring a 32 bit data whereas a 32-bit data bus would transfer the same in a single go.

- A bus clock decides how fast transactions can take place over the bus.

  - The bus clock rate is measure in MHZ.

Device Registers

- Device Registers are locations within a hardware device.

    - These locations can be read only, write only or both read and write.

    - The concept of device registers is analogous to registers within the microprocessor (AX, BX, CX. etc.).

- Moreover, a device can have more than one device registers.

    - In fact, real world devices usually have many device registers.

    - All device registers of a device occupy contagious addresses.

    - Devices therefore tend to work in a range of addresses where each individual device address in the address range corresponds to a single device register.

- The device registers of hardware devices are used for different purpose like

    - Transferring data.

- Obtaining status information of the device

- Controlling the behavior of the device.

Device Registers (Cont'd)

- Data registers are used for data transfer between the device and the CPU.

  - Device Drivers write data to output data registers.

  - Device Drivers read data from input device registers.

- The status device registers are read only and are read by device driver to obtain the status of the device.

  - For example, a device register in the printer would indicate the status of the printer (online / offline, paper empty, busy etc.)

- The control registers are used to control the functionality and behavior of the device.

  - Control registers usually write only and are written to by the device driver software.

  - For example, the control register of a device like printer can be used to start, abort data transfer or configure the device in some way.

Device Register Mapping

- Device drivers somehow need to access device registers.

  - Each device register of a device needs to be addressed uniquely just like locations within the memory chip.

  - Different processor architectures handle this situation differently.

- The x86 family of processor supports two types of addressing scheme memory-mapped I/O and port mapped I/O.

  - Under the memory-mapped I/O scheme, device registers of a hardware device are mapped onto location in the memory address space.

  - Under the port mapped I/O scheme device registers of a hardware device are mapped onto location in a separate address space knows as I/O address space.

Memory Mapped I/O

- The memory address space is simply a range of all valid memory address.

- The figure shows an example of a memory-mapped device the graphics display card.

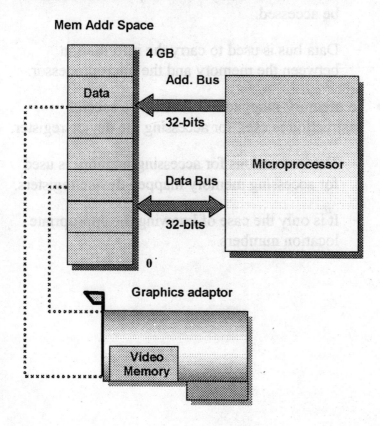

Mem Addr Space

Memory Mapped I/O (Cont'd)

- The video memory of the graphics adaptor card is memory-mapped in the memory address space.

  - Address bus is used to specify the location within the memory address space that needs to be accessed.

  - Data bus is used to carry the information between the memory and the microprocessor.

- In memory-mapped I/O scheme no special instruction is used for accessing the device register.

  - The instructions for accessing memory is used for accessing memory mapped device registers.

  - It is only the case of knowing the appropriate location numbers.

Port Mapped I/O

- The x86 architecture defines a separate address space known as "I/O address space" for mapping the device registers of devices.

  - Locations within the I/O address space are known as ports or port numbers.

  - A 16-bit address bus is used for accessing the locations within this I/O address space.

  - Data bus is used for transferring data between the locations and the CPU.

- In actual practice the data bus for memory address space and I/O address space is common.

  - Moreover the address bus for accessing I/O address space and memory address space is also common.

  - A dedicated line of the control bus is used to distinguish whether the address bus is being used for accessing the memory address space or I/O address space.

Port Mapped I/O (Cont'd)

- Figure shows a printer device connected to a D type 25-pin female connector. The device registers of the parallel port device are mapped in the I/O address space.

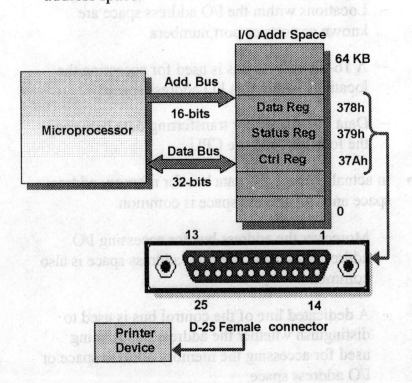

D-25 Female connector

Port Mapped I/O (Cont'd)

- The data, status and control registers of the parallel port device are mapped to locations numbers 378h, 379h and 37Ah.

  - Thus 378h, 379h and 37Ah are port address of 3 device registers of the parallel port device.

- The processor provides two separate instructions for reading and writing from/to the location in the I/O address space.

  - The **IN** instruction is used for reading from the device registers.

  - The **OUT** instruction is used for writing to the device registers.

Memory Vs. Port Mapped I/O

- How does a device manufacturer decide whether the device registers of the device have to be memory mapped or I/O mapped?

  - This depends upon the design and the nature of the device.

- Port-mapped device registers have the following characteristics.

  - Device registers have to be accessed with special processor instructions.

  - Accessing device registers using these instructions is slow as compared to memory access.

  - Only 16-bits of the 32-bit address bus can be used to address port mapped device registers.

  - A collection of device registers is knows as buffers.

  - Port mapping technique is only preferred for small sized buffers.

  - If a device has only a few device registers it will prefer using I/O mapped technique.

Memory Vs. Port Mapped I/O
(Cont'd)

- Memory-mapped device registers have the following characteristics.

- Any memory reference instructions can be used for accessing the memory mapped device registers.

  - While writing device drivers for NT this does not help in any way we still have to use the service provided by the HAL to access I/O mapped or memory mapped device registers.

- Not all processor architecture support I/O mapped and memory mapped techniques.

  - Some processors like Motorola only support memory mapped device registers there is no concept of I/O address space.

  - The internal implementation of the HAL routines automatically make use of the underlying facilities of the architecture to access the device registers.

- Devices that have many device registers (large buffer) usually are memory mapped.

- Accessing memory mapped device register is faster than I/O mapped device registers.

Device Register Addressing

- More often than not devices have more than one device register.

- Each device register has a unique location number either in the I/O address space or memory address space.

  - Thus a device tends to work in a range of address.

  - For example a parallel port device works in the range of 378h to 37Fh.

Trap

- The term trap refers to a processor's mechanism for capturing an executing thread when an exception or an interrupt occurs and transferring control to a fixed location within the OS.

  - This location is usually a routine known as trap handler, a function specific to a particular interrupt or exception.

- The following figure illustrates the working of the trap mechanism.

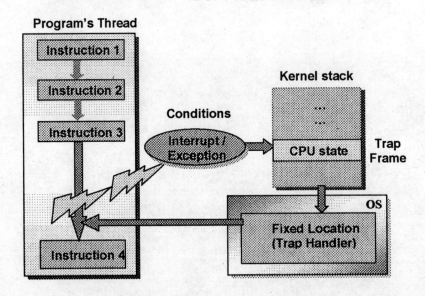

Trap (Cont'd)

- Figure shows a program's threads with a series of instructions.

- After the execution of the 3rd instruction is over an interrupt / exception occurs which cause the execution control to be transferred to a fixed location within the OS.

- Just before transferring the execution control to the OS the current state of the CPU (registers) are saved onto a kernel stack.

  - The saved state of the microprocessor (CPU) is often referred to as trap frame.

- When the trap handler finishes handling the interrupt / exception the CPU resumes its earlier activity by restoring its state from the trap frame.

Interrupts

- The trap handler for an interrupt is known as interrupt handler or Interrupt Service Routine.

- An interrupt is an asynchronous event that can occur at any given time.

  - The interrupt event generated by the I/O device is totally unrelated to the activity going on the system.

- Interrupts are largely generated by I/O device that need to seek the processors attention.

- Software programs can also generate interrupts.

- Interrupts can be enabled / disabled programmatically

- Hardware interrupts are usually non-reproducible

Exceptions

- The trap handler for an exception is simply known as exception handler.

- An exception is a synchronous event that occurs only at certain times.

- Exceptions are largely caused by the execution of program instructions.

- The exception event is highly related to the currently activity of the system

- Exception cannot be enabled or disabled programmatically

- Exception can be reproduced if the data and conditions required for the exception meet again

Reasons For Trap

- Both interrupts and exceptions can be caused by both hardware and software.

- Interrupts are largely caused by the hardware and exceptions are largely caused by software.

- Interrupts generated by hardware:

  - I/O device like keyboard for example generate interrupt when keys are pressed.

  - The in-built timer present on the motherboard of the compute also periodically generates an interrupt. In fact it is this interrupt that OS use to do the magic of thread scheduling.

- Exceptions generated by hardware:

  - The bus (ex PCI bus) may generate an exception if the device is not properly inserted in the expansion slots.

- Interrupts generated by software

  - Executing the INT instruction and specifying an interrupt number generate software interrupts.

- For example INT 2E instruction generates a software interrupt 2E that is used for making a system service calls (SSC).

- The kernel itself uses software interrupts to make a APC Asynchronous procedure call and a deferred procedure call (DPC)

Reasons For Trap (Cont'd)

- Exceptions generated by software:

  - The instruction which tries to divide a number by 0 generates a divided by 0 exception

  - The instruction which tries to read from an invalid memory location results into a memory access violation exception.

- Different trap handlers get called for different types of traps.

  - For example, if a type of trap is an interrupt then the corresponding interrupt service routine gets called.

  - If a system service call is made which issues software interrupt 2E the corresponding trap handler the system service gets called.

  - Hardware or software exception is tackled by an exception dispatcher routine, which further delegate the control to the registered exception handler routine.

  - Accessing an invalid virtual address location causes the corresponding trap handler (a virtual memory manager routine) gets called.

- All these different name are in fact nothing but
  name for the corresponding trap handlers

Device Signaling

- Device use some kind of signaling mechanisms for seeking CPU attention.

- The reasons for seeking CPU attention are as below

  - **Indicating ready state**: If a device has completed a previous I/O (read/write) operation and needs to indicate the system software that it is now ready for additional request it would simply send a signal to the CPU.

  - **Indicating overflow condition**: If the data buffer present on the device has become full during input/output the device needs to signal the system software to indicate the same so that the system software (device driver) know that it has to stop sending data to the device.

  - This condition is known as overflow condition.

  - **Indicating underflow condition**: Devices also need to take care of the underflow condition where the device buffer becomes empty during input/output and the device needs additional data in its buffer to continue.

  - **Indicating Error condition**: If the device encounters some error condition during an operation for example in the case of a printer if a paper gets jammed then the printer might need to inform the CPU (system software) by signaling it.

Signaling Priority

- The signaling mechanism used is interrupts.

- It is possible for more than one device to interrupt the CPU at the same time hence priority has to be taken care off.

  - The interrupt signals that the device generates are assigned priority values.

  - The device that can wait for some time to seek the attention of the CPU without losing its state or data is naturally assigned a lower priority.

  - Device that cannot wait are assigned higher priority.

  - Standard devices like keyboard printer, mouse, etc. are assigned fixed priority values that never change.

  - New and non-standard device are dynamically assigned priority values with the help of the HAL and PnP mechanism.

- If the microprocessor is busy servicing a lower priority interrupt a higher priority interrupt can still occur.

- – If such a thing happens the processor saves it state in the memory and continues with servicing the higher priority interrupt.

- – After servicing the higher priority interrupt the CPU automatically returns back to servicing the earlier (low priority) interrupt.

Signaling Priority (Cont'd)

- If however, the microprocessor is busy servicing the higher priority interrupt and a lower priority interrupt occurs then the corresponding device has to wait.

Interrupt Handling

- Different processor architectures employ different interrupt handling strategies.

- The techniques can be classified into two categories vector based and non-vector based.

- Non vector based interrupt handling has the following characteristics:

  - A common interrupt service routine ISR handles all interrupts.

  - The ISR on gaining control polls the list of interrupts in a priority order to figure out the interrupt number.

  - The technique is slower as compared to the vector-based method.

  - Only limited number of interrupts can be handled with this technique.

  - The time required to figure out which interrupt has occurred is not predictable and hence is not suited for real time processing.

- This technique is not so common. Modern processors architectures follow vector-based method of interrupt handling.

Interrupt Handling (Cont'd)

- Vector based interrupt handling has the following characteristics.

  - This technique makes use of a lookup table for handling interrupts.

  - Each interrupt has its own ISR and there is one to one correspondence with the interrupt number and the interrupt service routine.

  - This technique is mostly followed since interrupt dispatching is faster.

  - More number of interrupts can be handled with this technique

  - The time taken for interrupt dispatching is predictable and hence the vector based technique for handling interrupts is used for real time computing / processing.

Interrupt Handling (Cont'd)

- Slide show the interrupting mechanism used by device to seek the attention of the CPU and hence the system software (device driver).

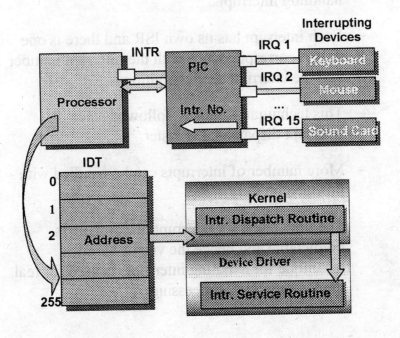

Interrupt Handling (Cont'd)

- The processor's IC has a pin called INTR that is connected to a programmable interrupt controller (PIC) usually an Intel IC 8259.

  - The IC is responsible for handling interrupt from different devices.

  - The different interrupting devices like keyboard mouse, sound card are connected to the PIC over lines known as I/O request lines (IRQ lines).

- When the device needs to signal the processor it produces a signal on the IRQ line.

  - The PIC in turn gets notified and in turn asserts (signals) the microprocessor on the INTR pin.

  - Note that different devices may simultaneously signal the PIC on different IRQ lines.

  - The PIC has some inbuilt prioritization scheme to handle this.

- Once the processor's INTR pin is asserted the processor saves its current state (register contents) and requests the PIC to obtain the interrupt number.

- The PIC converts the IRQL number to a suitable interrupt number and returns it to the processor.

- The processor uses the number obtained from the PIC to index into the interrupt descriptor table (IDT) to obtain the address of a routine that handles the interrupt.

Interrupt Handling (Cont'd)

- The corresponding routine is often known as Interrupt Service Routine.

  - The IDT is a table of all such address for different interrupt numbers.

  - Having obtained the address the CPU simply executes the machine code contained at that address.

  - This address happens to be the address of a kernel routine.

- The kernel routine does some house keeping job and calls the registered routine for handling the interrupt.

  - Device drivers usually register a routine (function) with the kernel for handling interrupt signals from the device.

  - Once the execution of the device driver routine ends the kernel gains control and ends the processing of interrupt in a platform specific way.

  - Once the interrupt signal terminates the processor resumes it earlier activity.

- If none of the device driver has registered a
  routine with the kernel, the kernel shoulders the
  responsibility of handling the interrupt.

- The mechanism whereby the kernel handles the
  before it reaches the device driver routine is know
  as front end interrupt handling.

Interrupt Priorities

- Hardware interrupt priorities are not consistent across different processor architectures.

  - This makes implementing the device driver code more difficult.

- NT abstracts the hardware priorities by implementing its own prioritization scheme.

  - NT prioritization scheme is known as IRQ levels (IRQL).

  - IRQL values range from 0 to 31.

  - 0 is the least priority level and 31 is the highest.

  - IRQL values are independent of the processor architecture and provide an abstraction for the priorities of both software and hardware interrupts.

  - Every code running on the system has to run at some IRQL value.

IRQL Levels

- The figure shows the details of each level IRQL level.

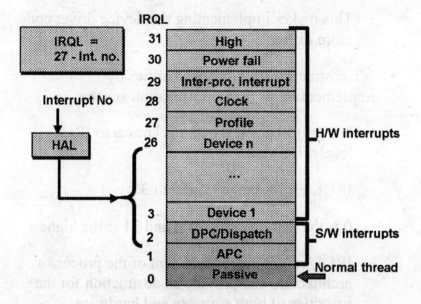

- IRQL level 0 is known as passive level.

    - All user mode application threads run at passive level.

    - In other words normal threading activity (thread switching) occurs at passive level.

- Once the IRQL level is raised above passive
  level the normal thread scheduling activity is
  stopped and current thread keeps executing till
  the time the IRQL value does not drop back to
  passive level.

- While the thread is running at IRQL value
  above passive level its activity can only be
  interrupt by a code running at still higher IRQL.

IRQL Levels (Cont'd)

- The IRQL values 1 and 2 are reserved for software interrupts.

- IRQL value 1 is used for Asynchronous Procedure Calls (APCs).

  - APC is a mechanism for executing some code in the context of a particular thread.

- IRQL value 2 is known as DPC/Dispatch level.

  - This level is used for Deferred Procedure Call (DPC).

  - This level is also known as dispatch level because thread dispatching occurs at this level.

  - We will see DPC in action in the next chapter.

- All the remaining IRQL values from 3 to 31 are reserved for hardware interrupts.

- The IRQL values from 3 to 26 are reserved for the hardware interrupts of different peripheral devices.

  - The HAL is responsible for mapping the interrupt number to the appropriate IRQL value.

- For the x86 architecture using PIC chip the HAL simply uses the formula 27 – interrupt number to obtain the corresponding IRQL number.

IRQL Levels (Cont'd)

- Changing the IRQL value is a highly technical task and is prohibited from user mode.

  - Only kernel mode code (thread) can change the IRQL value.

  - The kernel provides services like **KeRaiseIRQL( )** and **KeLowerIRQL( )** to raise and lower the IRQL value of the system.

- If the processor is currently executing code that is running at level n then all request for code running at level n and below will have to wait.

  - The low IRQL levels are said to be masked.

- DPC / Dispatch level (IRQL level 2) is special in that the code running at this level isn't allowed to perform a wait operation on synchronization objects.

  - Moreover the code isn't permitted to access non-paged memory

  - Deferred Procedure Calls (DPC) run at DPC / Dispatch level.

- The word deferred means that the execution of the routine (procedure) is delayed and is not immediately executed.

- Deferred procedure calls are extensively use to complete I/O requests from within ISR routine.

Data Transfer Techniques

- To transfer data between the device driver and the physical device different techniques like Programmed I/O (PIO), Direct memory access (DMA) and Shared buffers are used

    - Each technique has its own advantages and disadvantages.

- PIO technique is the most common technique used by devices that need to transfer only few bytes at a time.

    - This technique is the slowest as compared to other techniques however usage of this technique is the simplest.

    - Simple devices like parallel port, speaker ports make use of programmed I/O technique.

- DMA is a technique by which data transfer takes place between the main memory of the computer and the device without involving the CPU.

    - Since the CPU is not involved the speed of the data transfer increases significantly.

    - This mechanism is used by device that needs to rapidly transfer huge amount of data.

- – The implementation of this technique requires the use of a DMA controller, which is essentially a dumb processor.

Data Transfer Techniques (Cont'd)

- If the DMA controller circuitry is a part of the device then the device is said to have bus-mastering capability.

  - However, having bus-mastering capability increases the cost of the target device.

  - Simple devices therefore utilize the DMA controller available on the motherboard of the computer system. This mechanism is known as slave DMA.

  - Devices like hard disk, CD, network cards make use of DMA.

- Simply devices use the DMA controllers present on the motherboard and are known as slave DMA.

  - The motherboard has more than one DMA controllers for use by devices known as DMA channels.

- In shared buffers technique the memory present on the device is directly mapped into the memory address space.

  - Good example of such device is the video card and the ROM BIOS.

- This data transfer rate obtained with this technique is quit high.

Hardware Resources

- Each hardware device consumes some hardware resources.

- Hardware resource includes the following

  - **I/O range**: Devices consume a range of locations within the I/O address space for mapping their device registers.

  - **Memory Range**: Some device need a range of locations within the memory address space for mapping their device registers.

  - **Interrupts Request Line (IRQ)**: Interrupting device need to reserve the IRQ line on which they interrupt the microprocessor.

  - **Direct Memory Access (DMA) channels**: Slave DMA devices need to use DMA channels for transferring data.

- The hardware resource list for a device can be obtained from the device manager applet.

  - Open device manager by right clicking my computer icon on the desktop then select properties.

- Next select the hardware tab from the property sheet that appears and click device manager.

- From within the device manager window Right click the target device and select properties to view the complete list of hardware resources that the device is consuming.

Hardware Resources (Cont'd)

- The screen capture shows the hardware resource requirements for the printer port (LPT1) device.

Printer Port (LPT1) Properties

General | Port Settings | Driver | Resources

Printer Port (LPT1)

Resource settings:

Resource type	Setting
Input/Output Range	0378 - 037F
Interrupt Request	07

Setting based on: Current configuration

☑ Use automatic settings   Change Setting...

Conflicting device list:

No conflicts.

OK   Cancel

Summary

- Device has locations within them which can be read / written.

- These locations are known as device registers.

- Device registers are mapped to either IO address space or memory address space.

- Device registers mapped in the IO address space are said to be Port mapped and their access require use of special instructions

- Device registers mapped in the memory address space are said to be Memory mapped and their access doesn't require use of any special instructions.

- Interrupts are signaling mechanism used by devices to inform the CPU (system software) of critical events and errors.

- The 3 different techniques for data transfer used by devices are Programmed I/O, Direct Memory Access (DMA) and Shared Buffers.

Lab 5

Viewing Hardware Resources

Start the device manger applet from computer management applet. Observer the hardware resource requirements for device like mouse and keyboard.

Instructions:

- Open control panel.

- From the control panel select the system applet

- Select Hardware tab from the "system properties" property sheet.

- Click "Device Manager" button

- From the device manager window locate the keyboard device

- Right click the keyboard device and select properties from the context menu.

- Select the Resources tab from the property sheet

- Observe the hardware resource for the keyboard

- Repeat the same procedure for the mouse device

Chapter 6

Building Real World Drivers

Building Real World Drivers

Objectives

After completing this unit you will be able to:

- Understand many of the mechanisms used in real-world drivers.

- Understand how to handle interrupts from devices.

- Design a simple PIO device and write a real world driver for it.

Recap

- A device driver is basically a collection of different routines.

  - These routines are exported from the Device Driver and are called by the I/O subsystem on the occurrence of different events.

  - The routines are exported from the driver object. Fields present in the driver object hold the address of the different routines exported by the Device Driver.

- The *DriverEntry( )* also known as the initialization routine of a Device Driver is called by the I/O manager whenever the Device Driver is loaded into memory.

  - The *DriverEntry( )* routine is responsible for registering other routines of the Device Driver.

- *Unload* routine is called by the I/O manager whenever the driver is about to be unloaded from memory.

  - **Unload** routine is provided to do any cleanup activities like freeing up previously allocated memory.

- Dispatch routines are responsible for handling requests coming from the client or other drivers.

  - Dispatch routines run at **PASSIVE_LEVEL** and hence can easily access paged memory.

More Device Driver Routines

- A Device Driver may also implement routines like

  - Interrupt Service Routine

  - Deferred Procedure Call (DPC) Routine

  - Add-Device Routine

  - Start I/O Routine

- A short summary of these routines is presented below

- Interrupt Service Routine (ISR) is called whenever an interrupt occurs.

  - Every interrupt has its own Interrupt Service Routine.

  - Device Drivers typically register one or more interrupt service routines with the kernel for the handling hardware interrupts generated by the device they control.

  - Interrupt service routines are called at an elevated IRQL above **DPC/DISPATCH_LEVEL**.

- One must exercise caution while accessing
  resources like memory or data from within the
  ISR.

More Device Driver Routines

(Cont'd)

- Deferred Procedure Calls (DPCs) are functions that perform less critical activity than the activity that is currently going on.

  - These routines are called deferred since the execution of these routines is delayed (deferred) until the IRQL drops to **DPC/Dispatch** level.

- Sometimes, the activities that the Device Driver needs to carry out have to be delayed. The reasons for delaying the activities are as follows

  - Calling certain service function such as *IoCompleteRequest( )* is prohibited above DPC/Dispatch level.

  - Moreover, it is not advisable to keep the IRQL unnecessarily elevated at a higher level when that same activity can be performed at a lower IRQL.

- ISRs often need to complete IRP requests but are unable to do so since the ISR runs at quit a high IRQL level.

- The ISR normally requests a DPC routine for completing the IRP.

- Whenever the IRQL drops to **DPC/DISPATCH** level DPC software interrupt occurs and the pending DPC routine gets called which completes the IRP request on behalf of the ISR.

More Device Driver Routines
(Cont'd)

- The *AddDevice* Routine is a Device Driver exported routine that is called by the Plug and Play manager.

  - The PnP manager calls **AddDevice** routine of a device driver to indicate that a new hardware device was attached / found on the bus.

- Start I/O routine is an I/O manager provided feature for serializing multiple IRP requests coming from different client applications for the same device.

  - In a multitasking environment multiple clients can simultaneously invoke the routines of the device driver, which may cause adverse effects.

  - The I/O manager provides an automatic serialization of IRP requests for the device drivers.

  - All IRP requests are automatically placed in a queue, that are handled one by one by the Device Driver in its Start I/O routine.

The Parallel Port Device

- We propose to write a driver for a parallel port loop back device.

- Before we begin with discussing the details of the parallel port loop back device we need to understand how the parallel port device itself works.

- The parallel port device was explicitly designed to work with the printer device but it can be used for controlling simple devices also.

- The parallel port device features a 25-pin connector emerging at the backside of the CPU box.

  - 8 pins are used for output and 5 pins are used as input whereas 4 pins are used as bi-directional leads (both input and output).

- Each parallel port device has 3 device registers in it namely data, status and control.

  - The address of these device registers is port mapped and is in sequential order.

  - The address of the data register is also known as the starting address or the base address of the parallel port device.

- The status register immediately follows the data register and the control register follows the status register in the I/O address space.

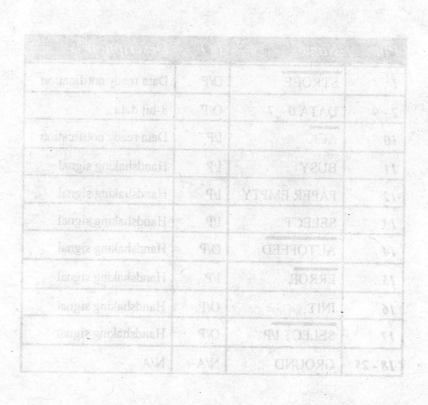

Pin Assignments

- The figure shows the pin assignments of the parallel port connector.

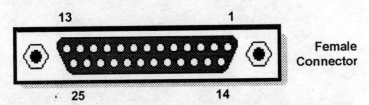

Female
Connector

Pin	Name	I/O	Description
1	STROBE	O/P	Data ready notification
2 - 9	DATA 0 – 7	O/P	8-bit data
10	ACK	I/P	Data ready notification
11	BUSY	I/P	Handshaking signal
12	PAPER EMPTY	I/P	Handshaking signal
13	SELECT	I/P	Handshaking signal
14	AUTOFEED	O/P	Handshaking signal
15	ERROR	I/P	Handshaking signal
16	INIT	O/P	Handshaking signal
17	SELECT I/P	O/P	Handshaking signal
18 - 25	GROUND	N/A	N/A

Pin Assignments (Cont'd)

- The parallel port connector is a 25 pin female connector seen at the back of the CPU box.

  - The parallel port is also known as the LPT port.

  - The printer cable is normally hooked up to the parallel port.

  - Pin no 1 is strobe. The line over the strobe indicates that the signal is active low and is read as "strobe bar".

  - Active low means that a 1 value (+5V) means that the strobe signal is off and a value of 0 (0V) means that the strobe signal is on.

  - Pin 2 – 9 is used as Data pins for transferring 8 bit data.

  - Similarly pins 11 – 17 are used for handshaking (communication) signals as used by the printer device.

  - Pins 18 – 25 are ground pins.

Device Register To Pin Mapping

- The figure shows the relationship of the three device registers with the 25 pin female connector.

  – Some of the bits of the device register remain unused.

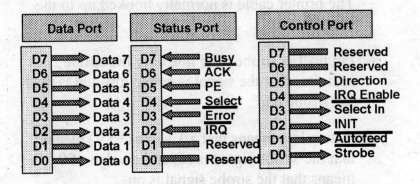

Data Port		Status Port		Control Port	
D7	Data 7	D7	Busy	D7	Reserved
D6	Data 6	D6	ACK	D6	Reserved
D5	Data 5	D5	PE	D5	Direction
D4	Data 4	D4	Select	D4	IRQ Enable
D3	Data 3	D3	Error	D3	Select In
D2	Data 2	D2	IRQ	D2	INIT
D1	Data 1	D1	Reserved	D1	Autofeed
D0	Data 0	D0	Reserved	D0	Strobe

Parallel Port Loop Back Device

- The figure shows the working principle of the parallel port loop back device.

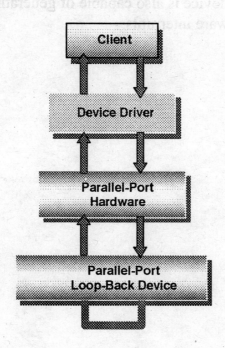

- The loop Back device is a simple device developed for checking the functionality of the parallel port device.

  - The loop back device would get connected on the parallel port connector.

- As the name suggests whatever data is sent by the driver to the device the device simply returns the same data back to the driver unchanged hence the name loop-back.

- The device is also capable of generating hardware interrupts.

Loop Back Device (Cont'd)

- The client application would establish a connection with the loop back device driver and then use *WriteFile( )* function to send some data to the device driver.

- The device driver would receive the request and send the same data to the parallel port device.

- The loop back device which itself is physically attached to the parallel port device would receive the data sent by the device driver and make the same data available to the parallel port hardware at a different location (pins).

- The device driver on receiving a *ReadFile( )* request from the client reads the data now available at the parallel port device and returns the same back to the client.

Loop back Device (Cont'd)

- The figure shows the internal structure of the parallel port loop back device for which we propose to write the driver.

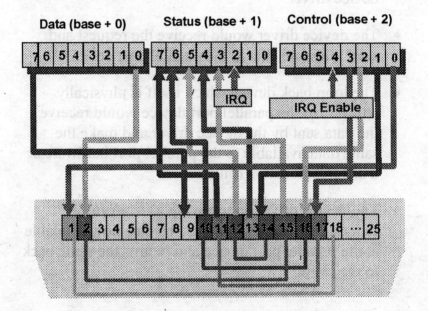

Loop back Device (Cont'd)

- This device can be created at home from a 25-pin parallel port male connector.

- All that has to be done is to connect the appropriate pins of the male connector as shown below

Pin number	Connects to
1	13
2	15
10	16
11	17
12	14

- The figure also shows how the device register bits are mapped to the pins of the loop back device.

  - The bit number 2 of the status register is IRQ and indicates whether interrupt has occurred or not.

- Bit number 4 of the control register is IRQ Enable and controls whether the parallel port device can generate interrupts.

- The bits marked with an X are unused.

Interaction With Loop Back Device

- The Loop back device is a programmed I/O device.

- The working mechanism of the device is illustrated in the following figure.

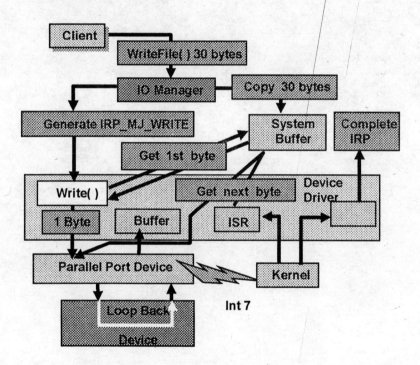

- The steps involved in writing and reading from the loop back device are as follows:

– The client initially makes a write request by using the *WriteFile( )* API. Let say that the client requests to write 30 bytes to the loop back device.

Interaction With LB Device (Cont'd)

- The loop back device is slow device and can only accept one byte at a time. The device driver for the loop back device has to implement a programmed I/O technique (PIO) to handle this situation.

- The *WriteFile( )* request reaches the I/O manager.

- The I/O manager firstly copies the 30 byte from the client buffer to a system buffer as a part of the Buffered I/O technique.

- The I/O manager then generates a IRP to represent the *WriteFile( )* request **(IRP_MJ_WRITE)**

- The I/O manager invokes the Dispatch routine for handling the **IRP_MJ_WRITE** request.

- The *Write( )* dispatch routine would make arrangements for accessing the system buffer and sending the very first byte of the system buffer to the parallel port device.

- The data reaches the loop back device since it is physically attached to the parallel port device and it loop backs the same data that it receives to a different set of pins

- The device driver then reads from these looped back pins and stores the data in its internal buffer.

- The device generates a interrupt to signal that it is ready to handle the next byte.

- The control reaches the kernel that hands over the control to the registered ISR routine.

Interaction With LB Device (Cont'd)

- The ISR routine accesses the 2nd byte from the system buffer and sends it to the parallel port device.

- The data is looped back as before and is read from the ISR and stored in the buffer.

- The device again generates an interrupt that causes the cycle to repeat till the time all the bytes have be transmitted and received in this fashion.

- Once the ISR figures out that all the byte have been processed it requests the kernel for a DPC routine.

- Once the IRQL level falls to level 2 the kernel calls the DPC routine, which completes the IRP request.

- Whenever the client makes a read request the device driver simply returns the contents of its buffer back to the client.

  - This mechanism of transferring data byte by byte to the client is known as Programmed I/O (PIO) and is used by slow device like printers scanners etc.

– The example although trivial helps us understand the PIO technique and the method of handling interrupts in a real world scenario.

Code Example

- In this section we would discuss the actual device driver code for the parallel port loop back device.

- A complete listing of the device driver can be found in the *Example\Chap06\loopback* directory.

String Handling

- Strings have to be represented mostly in Unicode format while working in kernel mode.

    - This requires working with **UNICODE_STRING** structure and specially designed kernel mode run-time library functions for manipulating strings.

    - Using this method every time string manipulation is needed makes the code unmanageable and increases the code listing.

- To make handling Unicode strings easier a user defined string-handling class has been designed.

    - The used of classes with overloaded operators makes string handling a lot easier in kernel mode.

    - The class is named **CString** and the source code of the string-handling library is present in **string.h** and **string.cpp** files.

    - The class has overloaded + and += operators for string concatenation.

Registering Entry Points

- The *DriverEntry( )* routine as usual registers the different entry points for the driver. The code snippet is shown below.

```
extern "C"
NTSTATUS DriverEntry ( PDRIVER_OBJECT pDrvObj,
                            PUNICODE_STRING pRegPath )
{
    DbgPrint ( "LoopBack: DriverEntry\n" ) ;
    NTSTATUS status = STATUS_SUCCESS ;
    pDrvObj->DriverUnload = Unload ;
    pDrvObj->DriverExtension->AddDevice = AddDevice ;
    pDrvObj->MajorFunction[IRP_MJ_PNP] = DispPnp ;
    pDrvObj->MajorFunction[IRP_MJ_CREATE] = Create ;
    pDrvObj->MajorFunction[IRP_MJ_CLOSE] = Close ;
    pDrvObj->MajorFunction[IRP_MJ_WRITE] = Write ;
    pDrvObj->MajorFunction[IRP_MJ_READ] = Read ;
    pDrvObj->DriverStartIo = StartIo ;
    return status ;
}
```

- Note that the *DriverEntry( )* routine registers a total of three new entry points namely *AddDevice*, *IRP_MJ_PNP* and *DriverStartIo*.

  - As said earlier the *AddDevice( )* routine is called whenever the PnP manager finds a new device on the bus.

- The **IRP_MJ_PNP** request is generated by the PnP manager for notifying the device driver of Plug and Play events taking place in the system.

- The I/O manger serializes IRP messages by calling the **DriverStartIo** routine.

AddDevice Routine

- Whenever a device is attached to the bus the corresponding bus driver detects the arrival of a new device on it.

  - Whenever the bus driver is loaded it enumerates the already attached devices on bus.

  - In both cases the bus driver reports the event to the PnP manager.

  - PnP manager loads the device driver for the detected hardware and calls the *AddDevice( )* routine.

- The first parameter of the *AddDevice( )* routine is the pointer to the driver object and the second parameter is the pointer to the Physical Device Object (PDO) that is created by the bus driver.

  - The device object created by the bus driver is known as Physical Device Object (PDO) since it directly communicates with the physical device

- PnP aware drivers always create device objects in the *AddDevice( )* routine.

  - The driver that we had created so far did not handle any PnP IRPs and were not PnP aware

and hence create their device objects in the
DriverEntry( ) routine.

AddDevice Routine (Cont'd)

- The *AddDevice* routine carries out the following series of operations.

- Dynamically construct a device object name.

  - If a system has 2 parallel ports then the PnP manager calls *AddDevice( )* routine of the each of the associated drivers twice.

  - This results in 2 device objects being created. The 2 device objects must definitely have unique names.

  - PnP aware drivers therefore construct device names dynamically like **\Device\LoopBack0**, **\Device\LoopBack1**, **\Device\LoopBack2** and so on.

- Create a Function Device Object (FDO).

  - A device can have more than one driver for its working.

  - Out of these, one of the drivers for a device is responsible for the working of the device and is known as function driver.

- The device object of the function driver is known as function driver object (FDO).

AddDevice Routine (Cont'd)

- While creating the device object the data transfer mechanism to be used between the client and the device driver has to be specified.

    - For the loop back device driver we have chosen the buffered I/O technique. The code snippet used for achieving this is shown below.

    ```
    pfdo->Flags |= DO_BUFFERED_IO ;
    ```

- Initializing the Device Extension Structure.

    - The device extension structure that got allocated during the creation of device object needs to be initialized with default values at this point. The device extension structure of the loop back driver is shown below.

    ```
    struct DEV_EXT
    {
        PDEVICE_OBJECT pDevObj ;
        PDEVICE_OBJECT pLowerDevObj ;
        ULONG DevNum ;
        CString DeviceName ;
        CString SymLinkName ;
        PUCHAR Buff ;
        ULONG BuffSize ;
        ULONG xferCount ;
        ULONG maxXferCount ;
    ```

```
        PUCHAR PortBase ;
        PKINTERRUPT pIntObj ;
        DEVICE_STATE state ;
} ;
```

AddDevice Routine (Cont'd)

- The different members of the device extension structure are as follows

  - **pDevObj**: contains the address of the device object of our driver.

  - **pLowerDevObj**: contains the address of the device object of the lower layered driver.

  - **DevNum**: contains the count of device objects created so far.

  - **DeviceName**: contains the name of this device object

  - **SymLinkName**: contains the symbolic link name of this device object.

  - **Buff**: contains a pointer to the data buffer for this device.

  - **BuffSize**: contains the size of the data buffer in bytes.

  - **xferCount**: contains a count of the bytes transferred so far.

- **maxXferCount**: contains a count of bytes to be transferred.

- **PortBase**: contains the base address of the parallel port device register.

- **pIntObj**: contains the address of the interrupt object used for registering interrupts.

- **state**: contain the PnP state of the device (started, stopped, removed).

AddDevice Routine (Cont'd)

- Attach the function device object to the existing stack of device objects for the parallel port device.

  - The loop back device gets attached to the parallel port device.

  - Hence the working of loop back device requires multiple drivers like parallel-port driver, port class driver, LoopBack device driver.

  - The device objects for these different drivers form a stack known as device object stack.

  - The I/O manager provides a service *IoAttachDeviceToDeviceStack( )* to attach the device object of a driver to the existing stack of device objects.

  - The service returns the address of the previous top of the stack device object.

  - This address has to be saved in the device extension structure of our driver. This address is referred to as the address of the lower device object.

- Having the address of the lower device object is necessary for communicating with the lower device driver.

AddDevice Routine (Cont'd)

- Create a symbolic link object.

    - Like the device object name the symbolic link name must also be constructed dynamically.

    - The symbolic link name that we have chosen is **\??\LOOP1, \??\LOOP2** and so on.

- Initialize the default DPC routine for the device object.

    - The I/O Manager provides a default DPC routine for every device object that gets created in the system.

    - Device Drivers make use of this default DPC routine for completing the IRP request from within the ISR by firing a DPC routine.

    - To be able to use the DPC routine it must be initialized. Initialization involves registering a user defined routine with the I/O manager using *IoInitializeDpcRequest( )* service.

AddDevice Routine (Cont'd)

- Lastly, the initializing status of the device object has to be removed.

  - The I/O Manager automatically removes the initializing status at the end of *DriverEntry( )* but not at the end of *AddDevice( )* routine.

  - This needs to be done manually by removing the bitwise flag **DO_DEVICE_INITIALIZING** from the **Flags** member of the device object structure.

Handling PnP notifications

- The dispatch routine for IRP_MJ_PNP handles the plug and play notifications sent by PnP manager.

  - The PnP manager sends notification messages in the form of IRP minor codes IRP_MN_xxx.

  - These notifications indicate a change in the PnP state of the device. The driver then accordingly takes the necessary steps.

  - The PnP minor codes are a part of the IO stack location structure of the current driver.

- The code for handling Plug and Play requests is shown below.

```
NTSTATUS DispPnp ( PDEVICE_OBJECT pdo,PIRP plrp )
{
    PIO_STACK_LOCATION plrpStack ;
    plrpStack = IoGetCurrentIrpStackLocation ( plrp ) ;
    DbgPrint ( "LoopBack: Received PNP IRP: %d\n",
                    plrpStack->MinorFunction ) ;
    switch ( plrpStack->MinorFunction )
    {
            case IRP_MN_START_DEVICE :
                    return StartDev ( pdo, plrp ) ;
            case IRP_MN_STOP_DEVICE :
                    return StopDev ( pdo, plrp ) ;
            case IRP_MN_REMOVE_DEVICE :
                    return RemoveDev ( pdo, plrp ) ;
```

```
        default :
            return PassDownPnP ( pdo, plrp ) ;
    }
}
```

Handling PnP notifications (Cont'd)

- The routine firstly obtains a pointer to the IO stack location structure of the current driver by calling the I/O manager service *IoGetCurrentIrpStackLocation( )*.

- The minor code is then extracted from the *MinorFunction* member of the structure.

- Depending upon the minor code obtained a different user defined helper routine is called to handle the request.

  - Each helper routine is passed the address of the device object and the pointer to the IRP structure.

  - Only 3 minor notification codes have been handled namely **IRP_MN_START_DEVICE**, **IRP_MN_STOP_DEVICE**, **IRP_MN_REMOVE_DEVICE**.

  - If any other minor code is encountered then we simply pass the IRP down to the lower layered driver. This has been accomplished by calling a user-defined routine **PassDownPnP( )**.

Passing IRPs Down The Stack

- The code for the PassDownPnP routine is shown below.

```
NTSTATUS PassDownPnP ( PDEVICE_OBJECT pdo, PIRP pIrp )
{
    IoSkipCurrentIrpStackLocation ( pIrp ) ;

    DEV_EXT* pDevExt = ( DEV_EXT * ) pdo->DeviceExtension ;

    return IoCallDriver ( pDevExt->pLowerDevObj, pIrp ) ;
}
```

- The routine calls the I/O manager service *IoCallDriver( )* to pass the IRP to the lower layered driver.

  - The first parameter of the service is the address of the device object of the lower layered driver. The address is available in the **pLowerDevObj** member of the device extension structure.

  - The second parameter of the service is a pointer to the IRP structure for the lower layered driver.

  - The pointer to the IRP structure of the lower layered driver is obtained by skipping the stack location by 1.

- – The I/O manager provides the *IoSkipCurrentIrpStackLocation( )* service for skipping the stack location by 1.

Starting The Device

- The *StartDev( )* helper function was called from the *DispPnP( )* dispatch routine on receiving a *IRP_MN_START_DEVICE* PnP code.

    - The PnP manager sends this code whenever the device needs to be started.

- In case of the loop back device we must register our ISR in the *StartDev( )* routine.

    - To register the Interrupt Service Routine (ISR) we must know lot of details regarding the interrupt.

    - This information can be obtained from the PnP manager.

    - The PnP manger provided information is deeply nested in a series of structures as shown in the figure below.

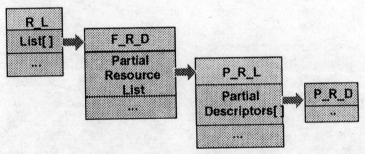

Abbreviation	Full Name
R_L	**PCM_RESOURCE_LIST**
F_R_D	**PCM_FULL_RESOURCE_DESCRIPTOR**
P_R_L	**PCM_PARTIAL_RESOURCE_LIST**
P_R_D	**PCM_PARTIAL_RESOURCE_DESCRIPTOR**

Starting The Device (Cont'd)

- The relationship of the structures is as below

  - The **PCM_RESOURCE_LIST** has an array member called list each of whose member points to **PCM_FULL_RESOURCE_DESCRIPTOR** structure.

  - The **PartialResourceList** member of this structure points the **PCM_PARTIAL_RESOURCE_LIST** structure.

  - The **PartialDescriptors** array within this structure further pointer to the **PCM_PARTIAL_RESOURCE_DESCRIPT OR** structure.

  - This structure finally contains a lot of technical information about the device in question.

  - **CM_RESOURCE_LIST** structure specifies all of the system hardware resources assigned to a device.

  - The count member of this structure for WDM compliant drivers is always 1.

- A **CM_FULL_RESOURCE_DESCRIPTOR** structure specifies a set of system hardware resources of various types, assigned to a device that is connected to a specific bus. This structure is contained within a **CM_RESOURCE_LIST** structure.

- The IRP stack location contains a parameters union that further contains a **StartDevice** structure, which contains **AllocatedResourcesTranslated** member that contains a pointer to the **PCM_PARTIAL_RESOURCE_DESCRIPTOR**.

Starting The Device (Cont'd)

- The *PCM_PARTIAL_RESOURCE_DESCRIPTOR* structure finally contains information that we want.

  - The **Type** member of the structure indicates the kind of resource for which the information is needed.

  - For the loop back device driver only the interrupt and port information is needed.

  - The **CmResourceTypeInterrupt** value indicates an interrupt resource type and **CmResourceTypePort** indicates an port resource type.

- For interrupt resource type the following information can be obtained.

  - **IRQL**: holds the IRQL value for the interrupt generated by the parallel port device.

  - **Vector**: holds the interrupt number. The interrupt number is used as an offset in the interrupt descriptor table

  - **Affinity**: holds the affinity mask value that decides which processor would handle the interrupt in a multiprocessor system.

- For port resource type the following information can be obtained.

  - Base address of the device registers.

Registering ISR

- To register the ISR we use the I/O manager provided service *IoConnectInterrupt( )* as shown in the following code snippet.

```
NTSTATUS status ;
status = IoConnectInterrupt ( &pe -> pIntObj, Isr, pe, NULL,
                    Vector, IRQL, IRQL, Latched,
                    TRUE, Affinity, FALSE ) ;
```

- The *IoConnectInterrupt( )* requires a lot of parameters which are discussed below.

  - The first parameter is the address of a KINTERRUPT structure (object) that would be setup with the appropriate values to represent the registered ISR.

  - **Isr** is the address of the routine which serves as the Interrupt Service Routine

  - **pe** is a user defined value to be passed to the Interrupt service routine. We have decided to pass the pointer to the device extension structure such that the ISR can access device specific information held in the device extension structure.

Registering ISR (Cont'd)

- **NULL** is a pointer to a spin lock object used for synchronization in case of multi processor systems. We have not specified a spin lock for out interrupt.

- **Vector** is the vector number for our interrupt that we wish to register.

- **IRQL** is the interrupt's IRQL value as decided by the HAL.

- **IRQL** is the level up to which the current IRQL must be raised in case of Sync Critical routine (discussed later).

- **Latched** indicates the interrupt mode latched / non-latched. The parallel port interrupt is a latched interrupt.

- **TRUE** indicates that the interrupt vector can be shared with other devices.

- **Affinity** specifies the affinity of this interrupt

- **FALSE** indicates that the floating-point status of the co-processor need not be saved on the stack whenever this interrupt occurs.

- Once the interrupt is successfully connected we pass the *IRP_MN_START_DEVICE* to the lower layered driver for further processing.

Stopping The Device

- The *StopDev( )* is a helper function that was called from the *DispPnP( )* dispatch routine in response to *IRP_MN_STOP_DEVICE*.

  - The PnP manager sends this minor code whenever it needs to stop the device.

  - For our loop back device we simply have to disconnect (un- register) the interrupt.

  - The I/O manager provides a service called *IoDisconnectInterrupt( )* for un-registering the ISR.

  - Finally, we need to change the state of the device to stopped state. The code snippet for achieving this is shown below.

```
NTSTATUS StopDev ( PDEVICE_OBJECT pdo, PIRP pIrp )
{
    DbgPrint ( "LB: StopDevice Handler\n" ) ;
    DEV_EXT *pe=( DEV_EXT * ) pdo->DeviceExtension ;
    if ( pe->pIntObj )
        IoDisconnectInterrupt ( pDevExt->pIntObj ) ;
    pe->state = Stopped ;
    return PassDownPnP ( pdo, pIrp ) ;
}
```

Removing The Device

- The *RemoveDev( )* helper function was called from the *DispPnP( )* dispatch routine in response to the *IRP_MN_REMOVE_DEVICE* minor code.

  - The PnP manager sends this code whenever the device is removed either physically or via the device manager.

- Removal of the device includes the following steps.

  - If the device is started, disconnect the interrupt.

  - Delete the symbolic link object and the device object.

  - Update the status of the device to removed status

  - Pass **IRP_MN_REMOVE_DEVICE** down to the lower layered driver such that the lower layered driver can also clean up any resources.

  - The code snippet for achieving this is shown below.

```
NTSTATUS RemoveDev (PDEVICE_OBJECT pdo, PIRP plrp)
{
        DbgPrint ( "LB: RemoveDevice Handler\n" ) ;
        DEV_EXT* pe=(DEV_EXT*)pdo->DeviceExtension ;
```

```
if ( pe->state == Started )
if ( pe->pIntObj )
        IoDisconnectInterrupt ( pDevExt-> pIntObj ) ;
UNICODE_STRING pLinkName=pe->SymLinkName ;
IoDeleteSymbolicLink ( &pLinkName ) ;
IoDeleteDevice ( pdo ) ;
pe->state = Removed ;
return PassDownPnP ( pdo, pIrp ) ;
}
```

Handling Write Request

- The code for *Write( )* dispatch routine is fundamentally different as compared to the driver that we have written so far.

  - The loop back device driver utilizes the IRP serialization facility provided by the I/O manager.

- Using the IRP serialization facility the device driver can handle multiple simultaneous IRP requests in an easy way without causing any synchronization problems.

  - Most device drivers that make use of the PIO mechanism for talking to their device utilize the IRP serialization mechanism.

  - This is because the PIO mechanism is a slow mechanism that takes quite some time and if in between the client makes another read / write request then the read / write dispatch routine might again get called before its execution is over thus leading to problems.

- Using the IRP serialization technique the IRP packet is simply marked as pending using the *IoMarkIrpPending( )* service.

- The packet is then placed in a queue for serialization and passed on to the *StartIO( )* routine for processing one by one.

- The *IoStartPacket( )* service helps us start processing the packet.

Handling Write Request (Cont'd)

- The *IoStartPacket( )* service requires several important parameters.

  - The first parameter required by the *IoStartPacket( )* is the address of the device object.

  - The second parameter is the pointer to the IRP to be routed.

  - The third parameter is a value that indicates the point where the IRP has to be inserted in the Queue (begin or end) 0 indicates the end.

  - The last parameter specifies the address of a cancel routine that is to be called if the IRP gets canceled.

- Lastly we return a pending status from the *Write( )* dispatch routine.

  - Asynchronously processing IRPs is useful for slower device that utilize the PIO technique for data transfer.

Cancel( ) Routine

- IRP packets can get cancelled if the application makes a call to the *CancelIo( )* API function.

  - The cancel routine is supposed to free up any allocated resources if any.

- The cancellation of an IRP requires the following steps.

  - Complete the IRP packet with a cancelled status

  - Proceed to process the next packet using the *IoStartNextPacket( )* service.

  - The *IoStartNextPacket( )* service begins by de-queuing the next packet form the queue and routing it to the *StartIo( )* routine.

Start I/O Routine

- *StartIo( )* routine is responsible for handling the IRPs that were serialized by the I/O Manager.

- The following series of steps are carried out from within the *StartIo( )* routine

  - If the function code for the IRP is **IRP_MJ_WRITE** then we simply note down the length of the write request as before, free up any previously allocated buffer, allocate a new buffer to hold the client buffer and copy the client supplied values in the newly allocated buffer.

  - If the allocation of the buffer fails then we complete the request with an error code to indicate insufficient resources and start to proceed the next packet

  - Next we begin to write the very first byte to the data register of the parallel port device by calling a user defined helper function *TransmitByte( )*.

- The *TransmitByte( )* function is however also called form the ISR.

- To avoid any synchronization problems of the *StartIo( )* routine with the ISR we makes use of the Sync Critical routine by calling the *KeSynchronizeExecution( )* service of the kernel.

- The Sync critical routine works by raising the IRQL value to that specified in the interrupt object and then calling the Sync critical routine.

Start I/O Routine (Cont'd)

- Now the ISR and the sync critical routine would work at the same IRQL value thus making sure that they cannot be run simultaneously on a single processor.

- If the execution of the sync critical routine fails due to any reason we simply fire a DPC routine to complete the IRP request.

- Lastly, if we receive any other IRP in the *StartIo( )* routine we simply complete the request with an unsupported IRP status and proceed to start the next packet.

Transmitting Bytes

- The *TransmitByte( )* helper function is responsible for transferring bytes to the actual physical device. The *TransmitByte( )* routine carries out the following steps

  - Check to see if all the bytes have been transmitted. If all the bytes have been transmitted then the routine simply returns a false value to indicate that the work is over.

  - Otherwise, the routine extracts next byte (for the first time this the very first byte) from the user buffer.

  - Write the 4 bits of the extracted byte to the loop back device using HAL services like *WRITE_PORT_UCHAR( )*.

  - The 4 bits of the next byte value that we want to write to the parallel port device's data register are not is sequential order.

  - The color-coding in the diagram helps us to understand the positions where we need to send the individual bits.

Transferring Bytes (Cont'd)

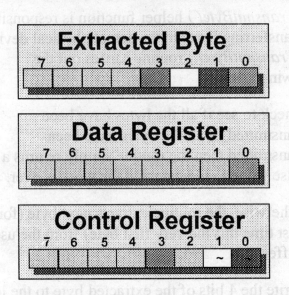

- The 4-bits of the extracted byte are marked in different colors and their destination position in the data register and control register are marked with the same color.

    - The ~ symbol indicates that the bits have to be complemented.

    - The 0th bit has to be written to the 0th bit of the data register as indicated by the blue colored square.

- The 1st and the 2nd bits have to be complemented and written to the 0th and the 1st bits of the control register.

- Lastly, the 3rd data bit has to be written to the 3rd bit of the control register.

Transmitting Bytes (Cont'd)

- After we write the 4-bit data to the loop back device the bits get looped back and are available in the status device register in as shown in the figure.

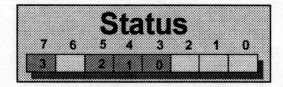

- The complete 8-bit value of the status register is read.

- Using bit-wise operators the 4-bits are then properly re assemble to form the 4bit value in the original form.

- The read value is copied to the data buffer.

- Generate an interrupt for transmitting the next byte.

- This is achieved by pulsing the RST bit of the parallel port device register device from 1 to 0.

- Firstly, we write a bit value containing the **IRQ_ENABLE** value, the RST value and the default mask. This has the effect of enabling interrupts and raising the RST bit of the control register.

– Then we introduce some delay by using the Kernel routine *KeStallExecutionProcessor( )*. The only parameter required by the service is the duration in microseconds.

Transmitting Bytes (Cont'd)

- Next we write the value IRQ_ENABLE and the default mask back to the control register. This time there is not RST bit which means the RST bit will be written with a 0 value as a result the RST bit will go down from 1 to 0.

- The RST bit of the loop back device is looped back to an appropriate pin on the parallel port that generates an external hardware interrupt.

Handling Interrupts

- The Interrupt service routine is called whenever the device generates an interrupt.

  - The first parameter received by the ISR is the pointer to the interrupt object

  - The second parameter is service context a user defined value that we specified when we registered the ISR during the *IoConnectInterrupt( )* call.

  - We had specified a pointer to the device extension as the user defined value for the ISR.

- The ISR performs the following steps

  - Read the status device register of the parallel port device.

  - Check the STS_IRQ bit of the read byte to see if an external interrupt has occurred or not.

  - If an external interrupt has not occurred then simply return a false value from the ISR.

  - Transmit the next byte of data by calling the *TransmitByte( )* helper function.

- If the *TransmitByte( )* routine indicates an error because all the bytes have been successfully transfer and it cannot further trasmit bytes a DPC is requested by using the I/O manager service *IoRequestDPC( )*.

Handling Interrupts (Cont'd)

- The DPC routine is responsible for completing the IRP request

- Lastly we return a true value to indicate that the interrupt was successfully processed.

- Note that the DPC routine is not called immediately it is deferred till the time the IRQL value does not fall to the DPC / Dispatch level.

Completing The Request

- The DPC routine is requested from 2 different places in the program.

  - **From within StartIo( ) routine**: The DPC routine is directly called if the sync critical routine fails or if the *TransmitByte( )* function returns an error.

  - **From within the ISR**: If all the bytes have been transmitted then the *TransmitByte( )* returns an error and the DPC routine is indirectly called by firing a DPC request.

- The DPC routine is simply used for completing the *IRP_MJ_WRITE*.

  - Note that the ISR cannot call the *IoCompleRequest( )* service since it executes at an elevated IRQL.

  - Hence we issue a deferred procedure call and then complete the IRP request form within the DPC routine.

  - While completing the request on behalf of the ISR we specify a value of **IO_PARALLEL_INCREAMENT** for boosting the priority of the client thread in order to compensate for the time it spent waiting for the transaction to be finished.

- The IO_PARALLEL_INCREAMENT is a standard value used for parallel port device.

- If the DPC routine was called as a result of the failure of the sync critical routine we simple complete the request without boosting the priority of the client thread.

- Lastly, the execution of the next IRP packet (if any) is started.

Deploying The Driver

- To install the driver we have to make some entries in the registry. As usual we have written a registry script to automate our task of installation.

- The script code is shown below

```
REGEDIT4
[HKEY_LOCAL_MACHINE\System\CurrentControlSet\Services
                    \LoopBack]
"Start" = dword : 3
"Type" = dword : 1
"ErrorControl" = dword : 1
"DisplayName" = "Parallel Port LoopBack Device Driver"

[HKEY_LOCAL_MACHINE\SYSTEM\CurrentControlSet\Control
    \Class\{4D36E978-E325-11CE-BFC1-08002BE10318}]
"UpperFilters" = "LoopBack"
```

- Note that the start type of the loop back driver is kept as 3, which means the driver would be loaded on demand.

  - The driver would be automatically loaded when the system bus finds the parallel port attached during enumeration.

Deploying The Driver (Cont'd)

- The last three lines of the script mark the driver as an upper filter driver for the parallel port class driver.

  - The 4D36E978-E325-11CE-BFC1-08002BE10318 is a class GUID (Globally unique identifier) for the parallel port device.

  - We register our driver as an upper filter class driver. Since our driver will be an upper filter driver the driver would receive all IRP requests first.

  - Note that although the driver is deployed as a filter driver it still acts like a function driver.

- Lastly we need to configure the parallel port device to generate interrupts.

  - By default the parallel port device does not generate any interrupts. We need to change this default setting.

  - Open computer management (Right click my computer select manage) browse device manager and select the properties of the printer port (LPT1) device. Click the Port Settings Tab and select the option "Use any interrupt assigned to the port".

- This will enable the parallel port device to generate interrupts.

Testing The Driver

- To test the driver follow the steps as given below

  - Build the driver

  - Plug in the loop back device to the parallel port

  - Double click the .reg file

  - Reboot the system

  - Run the test program in the
    Chap06\loopback\Test directory

Summary

- A driver handles the Plug and Play notifications by implementing a dispatch routine for the *IRP_MJ_PNP* request.

- The IRP_MN_xxx minor codes indicate the exact Plug and Play notification messages as sent by the PnP manager.

- I/O manager provides a default IRP serialization facility of each individual device object in the system.

- The device driver is required to mark an IRP pending by calling *IoMarkIrpPending( )* and then start the packet by calling *IoStartPacket( )* to serialize IRP requests.

- A sync critical routine is a synchronization mechanism used by device driver to synchronize access to routine called from the ISR and normal routines.

- Device Drivers register Interrupts routines with the kernel using I/O manager service *IoConnectInterrupt()*.

- DPC routines can be request by calling *IoRequestDPC( )* service.

- DPC routines are called when the IRQL value drops down to *DPC/Dispatch* level.

Lab 6

Driver for loop back device

Implement the device driver program for the loop back device discussed in the class. Ensure that the nibble sent to the loop back device is rotated by one position to the right before returning it back.

Suggested time: 60 minutes

Answers Directory: Chap06\loopback

Files: loopback.cpp, cstring.cpp, cstring.h, makefile, sources, install.reg

Instructions:

- Create the driver program, source file, makefile and install.reg script as per the loopback example covered in the chapter.

- Modify the TransmitByte( ) function so that the looped back data is shifted by 1 position before it is stored in the internal buffer.

- Build the driver.

- Plug in the loop back device.

- Deploy the driver using registry script.

- Reboot the system.

- Run the client application located in the
  Examples\loopback\Test directory.

- Verify that the client application runs successfully
  by interpreting the console messages.

Chapter 7

Bus Architectures

Bus Architectures

Objectives

After completing this unit you will be able to:

- Understand different bus architectures.

- Understand how bus architectures affect the design of device drivers.

- Understand how buses provide plug and play support.

- Understand different interrupt signaling mechanism used by various bus architectures.

Overview Of Bus

- A bus is the means for devices to get connected to the microprocessor.

    - A bus is simply a collection of parallel wires that constitute of data, address and control signal lines.

- The bus width dictates how much data can be transmitted on the bus in a single go.

    - The width of the bus is the number of lines available on the bus.

    - Bus that have more number of line allow multiple bits of data and control signals to pass in a single go.

    - Some buses constitute of a single wire through which data and other information pass in a serial fashion one bit at a time.

- Almost every different bus has its own way of communicating with the device attached to it.

    - Some bus architectures directly allow a device to communicate with other device attached on the same bus.

- Some bus architecture enforce that a device firstly communicate with a master or I/O controller.

- The I/O controller communicates with the target device on behalf of the first device.

Overview Of Bus (Cont'd)

- Windows 2000 / XP and future versions of the NT family easily support new bus technologies.

  - If a new bus comes along the way these OS require that only a bus driver be installed and the bus starts functioning.

  - Earlier versions of NT OS required a modification in the HAL layer whenever newer bus architecture was to be supported.

- Buses become popular and obsolete along with time. The main factors that decide the popularity of bus are as follows.

  - **Speed** – The rate at which the bus can transmit data or information. The higher the better.

  - **Cost** – The cost of implementing the bus technology. The lower the better.

  - **Ease of Use** – Probably one of the biggest factors is the ease of use for the end user.

  - Plug and unplugging of devices on the bus should be easier for the typical end user. For example some bus architectures permit devices to be plugged and unplugged without requiring a

system reboot or without causing any electrical
damage.

Bus Architectures

- The table shows some of the bus architecture in existence along with their full names.

Bus Name	Full Name
ISA	Industry Standard Architecture
EISA	Extended ISA
PCI	Peripheral Component Interconnect
AGP	Accelerated Graphics Port
PCMCIA	PC Card Bus
IEEE 1394	Fire Wire Bus
USB	Universal Serial Bus

Hardware Resources Conflicts

- Every hardware device attached to the system consumes resources.

- A list of different hardware resources is discussed below.

  - **I/O Range**: The device registers of a device may be mapped into the I/O address space, which would consume some locations within the I/O address space.

  - **Memory Range**: A memory-mapped device consumes a range of locations in the memory address space.

  - **Interrupt Request**: Interrupting device needed IRQ lines to interrupt the microprocessor.

  - **DMA**: Device that use slave Direct Memory Access (DMA) consume DMA channels.

- Conflict occurs when more than one device tries to use the same resource.

  - Hardware resources are limited. For example the number of IRQ lines available on the system is very less.

- Different devices manufactured at different times by different vendors often cause inevitable resource conflicts.

- For example, two devices may try to use the same IRQ line for interrupt the microprocessor exclusively.

Resolving Conflicts

- To avoid these conflicts earlier devices made use of manual configuration via jumpers and DIP-switches.

    - Jumpers are similar to toggle switches

    - DIP stands for Dual Inline Package and is a kind of switch.

    - These switches are present on the device itself and permit manual configuration of the device.

- This solution however is unrealistic since it requires the end user to have technical knowledge about the device.

    - Moreover, manual configuration may result in errors.

    - Unresolved conflicts may lead to an unbootable system or an unusable device.

- Modern solution to this problem is the use of Plug & Play technology.

Plug and Play

- PnP is a technology that enables a computer system to recognize and adapt to hardware configuration changes with little or no intervention by a user.

  - A user can add devices and remove devices from a computer system without having to do awkward and confusing manual configuration, and without having knowledge of intricate computer hardware.

  - PnP requires support from the bus, device hardware, system software, and drivers.

- Initiatives in the hardware industry define standards for easy identification of add-in boards and basic system components.

  - For example Plug and play support is provided for different bus architectures like PnP ISA, PCI and USB buses.

- The system software support for PnP, together with PnP drivers provides the following

- Automatic and dynamic recognition of installed hardware:

- The system software recognizes hardware during initial system installation, changes that occur between system boots and responds to run-time hardware events such as docking or undocking and device insertion or removal.

Plug and Play (Cont'd)

- Hardware Resource Allocation and Re-allocation:

  - The PnP manager determines the hardware resources requested by each device (for example, input/output ports (I/O), interrupt requests (IRQs), direct memory access (DMA) channels, and memory locations and assigns hardware resources appropriately.

  - The PnP Manager reconfigures resource assignments when necessary, such as when a new device is added to the system that requires resources already in use.

  - Drivers for PnP devices do not assign resources; instead, the requested resources for a device are identified when the device is enumerated.

  - The PnP Manager retrieves the requirements for each device during resource allocation.

- Loading of appropriate drivers

  - The PnP Manager determines which drivers are required to support each device and loads those drivers.

- A programming interface for drivers to interact with the PnP system.

  - The interface includes I/O manager routines, Plug and Play IRPs, required standard driver routines, and information in the registry.

Plug and Play (Cont'd)

- Mechanisms for drivers and applications to learn changes in the hardware environment and take appropriate actions.

  - PnP enables drivers and user-mode code to register for, and be notified of, certain hardware events.

- Plug and Play requires support from device drivers

  - For a driver to qualify as PnP it must provide the required PnP entry points, handle the required PnP IRPs and follow PnP guidelines.

- For devices to support PnP they must support auto recognition and auto configuration.

  - Auto recognition requires that the device must report its presence to the system software and also uniquely identify itself when asked for.

  - Auto configuration requires that the device report a lot of information about itself known as the resource list to the system software.

  - Resource list involves the manufacturer name, device type, I/O range requirements, memory

range requirements, interrupt request line
requirements and DMA channel requirements.

- The device should also be able to reconfigure
  the usage of its resources dynamically.

Plug and Play (Cont'd)

- Plug and Play system is divided into two categories cold and hot.

  - The cold variation requires that the system be rebooted so that the system takes note of the device attached.

  - Whereas the hot variation does not require a reboot.

  - Hot plug able devices improve the ease of use for a typical end user.

  - Not all bus architectures support hot variation of plug and play.

Interrupt Signaling

- Interrupts are signaled to the microprocessor using one of the two signaling mechanisms.

  - Edge triggering

  - Level triggering

- The figure discusses the edge-triggered interrupt signaling mechanism.

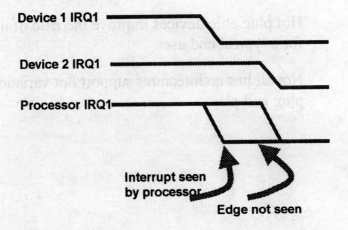

- An edge-triggered interrupt line signals an interrupt only when it sees a transition from the "unasserted state" to the asserted state.

Interrupt Signaling (Cont'd)

- As shown in the figure, a device holds the interrupt line. As long as the line is held down no other device on the line can generate a transition until the line is released.

- If another device tries to interrupt the processor at this stage the interrupt goes unnoticed by the processor.

- Thus, devices cannot share edge-triggered interrupt lines.

- ISA bus uses the edge triggered signaling mechanism and hence cannot share interrupts.

- A level triggered interrupt repeats as long as the interrupt line remains asserted.

  - Each time the processor becomes interruptible at that IRQL, and the IRQ line is asserted, the interrupt will occur.

  - The ISR must dismiss the interrupting device before returning. The following figure shows how level triggered interrupts work.

Dev1 IRQ1

Dev 2 IRQ1

IRQ1 Line

DIRQL 1

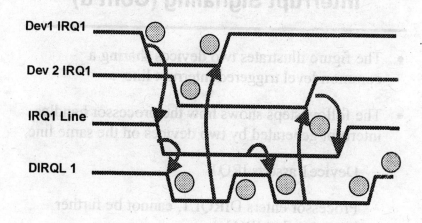

Interrupt Signaling (Cont'd)

- The figure illustrates two devices sharing a common level triggered interrupt line.

- The follow steps shows how the processor handles interrupt generated by two devices on the same line

  - Device1 asserts IRQ1

  - Processor enters DIRQL1, cannot be further interrupted at IRQ1.

  - Device2 asserts IRQ1

  - ISR for Device clears interrupt condition.

  - ISR returns from DIRQL1, processor becomes interruptible.

  - Because IRQL1 is still asserted by Device2, processor interrupts again.

  - ISR for Device2 clears interrupt condition.

  - ISR returns from DIRQL1, processor becomes interruptible

  - IRQL1 not asserted, no interrupt.

Hardware Enumeration

- The PnP manager enumerates the different hardware device attached to the system.

  - The PnP manager starts with a root device that is responsible for detecting non-plug and play device attached to the system.

  - Non-plug and play devices are devices that cannot electronically announce their presence to the system.

  - The root device takes the help of the information that setup program generated by running a hardware detection program.

- The following figure illustrate such an enumeration processes.

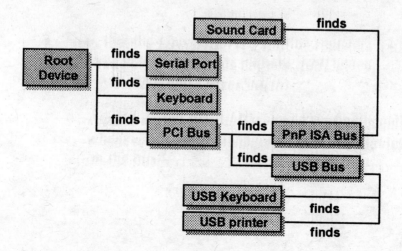

Hardware Enumeration (Cont'd)

- Lets say that the root device found the serial port, the keyboard and the PCI bus.

- The drivers for these devices are then loaded.

- The driver for the PCI bus (the PCI bus driver) further finds the ISA bus and the USB bus attached to it and reports it to the PnP manager.

- Each of these bus further find the devices attached to them.

- This recursive hardware enumeration leads to the formation of what is known as the device tree.

ISA Bus

- The ISA bus was originally designed by IBM for the PC/AT system and is now more than 2 decades old.

- The ISA bus only supports 8 bit and 16 bit devices.

- The ISA bus does not offer high-speed data transfers and is not very simple to interact with.

  - The clock speed for the ISA bus is only 8.33 MHz.

  - Moreover a 16-bit transfer on the ISA bus takes up two clock cycles.

  - The maximum data transfer rate for the ISA bus is 8 MB/sec.

  - The current CPU speed is two orders of magnitude faster than the speed offered by the ISA bus and hence is no longer a relevant bus.

  - However the ISA bus is still used for connect very simple devices.

  - Windows still supports the ISA bus for backward compatibility.

- − New motherboards do not have the ISA bus.

- − The ISA bus usually is identified by its color, which is black.

- The ISA bus does not support auto-recognition and auto-configuration of device attached to it.

  - − The ISA bus is a perfect example of non-plug and play hardware.

ISA Bus (Cont'd)

- The ISA bus specification does not dictate any rules for device register usage.

  - Device may grab any I/O address.

  - The only rule enforced is that the device present on the motherboard utilizes the range 0000h – 00ffh while the plug in cards make use of the 0100h – 03ffh.

  - Each plug in card on the ISA bus is assigned a 32-byte contiguous range of register access but the starting address of this address range is not defined.

- Legacy ISA cards tend to pose more problems as they cannot fully decode all the 16 address lines in the I/O address space

  - Legacy ISA cards can only decode 10 lines out of 16.

  - The end result is that the device responds to alias address in multiples of 0x400.

  - For example, a device that normally responds at location 300h would also respond at location

700h. This second address is know as an alias address of the first.

– Address aliases cause the I/O address range to diminish very quickly which is bad because other device on the system would not get locations in the I/O address space as would be rendered useless

ISA Bus (Cont'd)

- Interrupts are handled on the ISA bus by a pair of Intel 8259 PIC (Programmable Interrupt Controller chip) or an equivalent chip that emulates 8259.

    - Each PIC chip is capable of handling only 8 interrupt lines and hence provides only 8 levels of interrupt priority.

    - Devices interrupt the PIC and the PIC in turn interrupts the microprocessor.

    - In other words, the PIC multiplexes 8 interrupt lines to a single line.

    - 2nd line of the 1st PIC chip is connected to the 2nd PIC to route interrupts.

    - Thus a total of 16 lines from 2 PIC chips are multiplexed to 1 line of the microprocessor.

    - One of the lines is used for cascading the two PIC chips. So devices can use a maximum of 15 interrupt lines.

    - The 8259 PIC chip supports both edge / level triggered interrupts i.e. the chip can be programmed to either listen for edge / level triggered interrupts not both.

- The 8259 PIC cannot be programmed on a line by line basis giving the capability to listen for edge triggered interrupt on one line an level triggered interrupt on the other line.

ISA Bus (Cont'd)

- ISA uses the 8259 PIC in the edge-triggered mode.

- Moreover the IRQ lines used by the ISA bus cannot be shared amongst devices.

- A pair of 8237 DMA-controller IC handles DMA for the ISA bus.

  - Each DMA chip provides 4 independent channels. The channel numbers are numbered starting from 0.

  - A standard configuration cascades the two chips connecting the master (first) DMA chip to channel 1 of the 2nd chip.

  - The 1 channel is lost in cascading the two chips, which leaves 7 free channels for the use of devices. So out of the total 8 DMA channels (DMA channels 0 to 7) channel 4 is lost in cascading the two chips.

  - The upper channels (channels 5, 6 and 7) of the slave IC can transfer data at twice the rate of lower channels (channels 01 to 3) of the master DMA IC. This is because the slave DMA channels transfer only 16 bits at a time.

- ISA bus has only 24 address lines that limit the total amount of memory that can be transferred to a maximum of 16MB.

- If the DMA channels are in simultaneous use then the DMAC follows a software prioritization scheme in which highest priority is given to channel 0 and the lowest priority is given to channel 7.

EISA Bus

- The EISA bus is basically an extension to the old ISA standard.

- The EISA supports various data transfers sizes of 8 bits 16 bits and 32 bits.

- The EISA can support a maximum of 32 MB/sec data transfer rate.

- The EISA is designed to be fully backward compatible with the ISA bus.

  - The clock speed of the EISA bus remains 8 MHz, which is same as that of the ISA.

  - EISA slots are designed so that they can accepts old ISA cards as well as the new EISA cards

- The EISA bus can support a maximum of 15 slots which each slot having a fixed 4KB I/O address space.

  - This increase in the I/O space is an attempt to minimize the port resource conflict that arises due to limited I/O address space.

- The ISA and EISA have an address aliasing problem so only 256 bytes of register address space is guaranteed to be unique.

EISA Bus (Cont'd)

- The EISA also supports auto configuration of devices attached to it.

- EISA interrupt handling is basically a superset of the ISA interrupt-handling scheme.

  - EISA interrupt controllers provide the same 15 levels available on the ISA bus.

  - Each IRQL line can be individually programmed for edge-triggered / level – sensitive operation.

  - This arrangement allows both ISA and EISA cards to coexist on the same bus

- The DMA handling capability of the EISA bus is mostly same as that of the ISA bus.

  - A pair of 8237 DMAC chips is cascaded to provide 8 DMA channels numbered from 0 through 7. Channel number 4 as in the case of ISA is lost in cascading the 2 chips.

  - Unlike ISA the DMAC chips of EISA bus support the data transfer of 8 bits / 16 bits or 32 bit by any of the 7 available channels thus any device can use any channels.

- A special 24-bit count register supports a single transfer to reach up to 16MB of memory. The DMAC can also be programmed to use a 16-bit count register.

- The EISA DMA also supports full 32 bit address so that it can transfer data to and from the entire 4 GB address space.

EISA Bus (Cont'd)

- The EISA configuration process involves the following steps.

  - First, each card is required to implements a 4-byte ID register at location 0xnC80, where **n** is the EISA slot number from 1 to Ah.

  - The ID register identifies the manufacturer, the device type and the revision level of the card placed in that slot.

  - Second, designers can use the remaining 124 bytes (from nC84h to nCFFh) to implement other registers that configure the card.

  - For example, there might be a configuration register for the DMA channel number the card should use, and another for setting its IRQ level.

  - Storing values into these registers is equivalent of setting DIP-switches and jumpers on legacy ISA cards.

  - The third component is a script file that contains the card's resource list and defines the location and usage of any device-specific configuration registers on the card.

- This file is written in a standard EISA scripting language and is based on the contents of the card's ID register.

- This script usually comes on a floppy disk supplied by the cards manufacturer.

EISA Bus (Cont'd)

- The last component of the EISA configuration is a program that runs when a system boots. The program scans the EISA slots, looking for cards in previously empty locations.

- If it finds one, it uses the contents of the slot's ID register to construct the name of a configuration script and then asks the user for the floppy containing the script.

- Once the disk is inserted, the configuration program assigns resources to the card.

- The program also copies these assignments to nonvolatile CMOS memory associated with the slot, so it won't be necessary to ask for the script file with each boot.

PCI Bus

- The PCI bus is often the main bus of the system.

  - Every other bus connects to the PCI bus.

- The PCI bus was designed for carrying data at high speed.

  - Network cards, full motion video cards that have 24/32 bits per pixel displays require such high-speed buses.

  - The initial bus clock speed of the PCI bus was 33 MHz. This means that 33 * 1024 *1024 clock cycles complete at one second.

  - The bus can transfer data on every cycle. More recent PCI buses support 66 MHZ and above

  - The PCI bus often uses some clever optimizations such as burst mode and read ahead cache in which it can transfer data on the rising as well as the falling edge of the clock pulse that makes it possible for the PCI bus to achieve a maximum of 132 MB / sec data transfer rate for 32-bit transfers and 264MB/sec for 64bit transfers.

- The architecture of the PCI bus is processor neutral.

- The PCI bus supports the Alpha DEC and PowerPC platforms apart from the x86.

PCI Bus (Cont'd)

- Up to a maximum of 32 physical devices can be attached to a single PCI bus.

  - Each physical device can contain a maximum of 8 functional units within it.

  - A function unit in a device is a mini device.

  - For example a CD-ROM device features an in built Audio player. This inbuilt audio player is the function unit within the CD-ROM device.

  - Up to a maximum of 255 functional units can be attached to a single PCI bus.

  - According to the PCI Specification a maximum of 256 different PCI buses can be attached to a single computer system.

  - Although most computer system available today only feature a single bus.

- The PCI bus supports the direct communication of one device to another.

USB Bus

- The USB bus has the best Plug and Play support available.

  - USB supports both cold and hot PnP support.

  - That is whenever a new device is connected to the bus a reboot is not required to configure the device.

  - Similarly, it is not necessary to shut down the system to remove an already attached device on the bus.

  - The USB bus is specially designed so that plugging and unplugging devices on the bus (while the system is running) does not cause any electrical damage to the device or the bus or the system in any way.

  - Device attached to the USB bus can electronically identify themselves. This is necessary in order to fully comply with the PnP system.

- The USB features a special plug that consists of a 4-wire conductor that either connects to the PC or to the HUB device.

- A hub is a device to which USB devices can plug in.

- At least one hub is present in every USB system, which is often known as the root hub.

- The 4-wire used in the bus are as follows **Transmit (Tx)**, **Receive (Rx)**, **Power** and **Ground**.

USB Bus (Cont'd)

- USB features only a single wire to send / receive data.

  - The data transfer takes place in a serial fashion bit by bit.

- USB devices vary in speed.

  - Some device work at lower speed and some work at higher speed.

  - The USB bus supports both high speed and low speed devices.

- The USB bus supports daisy chaining of devices.

  - Up to a maximum of 127 different devices can be chained and attached to a single USB bus.

Summary

- Bus is the means by which devices get connected to the microprocessor.

- Bus provides support for plug & play, interrupt signaling, and DMA data transfers for devices.

- The recursive hardware enumeration results in a tree called device tree.

- Any imaginary root bus is responsible for detecting most of the non-plug and play devices present on the motherboard.

- The PCI bus is the master bus on the system. Every other bus connects to the system via the PCI bus.

- Buses connect to each other via bridge devices. For example, a "PCI To ISA Bridge" device helps connect the ISA bus to the PCI bus.

- Devices cannot share edge-triggered interrupt lines. Whereas devices can safely share a level-triggered interrupt line.

- Hardware resources includes Input Output range, memory range, interrupt request and DMA channels.

- **The Plug and Play manager resolves hardware resource conflicts.**

Lab 7

Viewing Device Tree

Start the device manager applet from the control panel and watch the formation of the device tree for your system.

Suggested time: 30 minutes

Instructions:

- Open Control panel.

- From the control panel select the system applet.

- Select the Hardware tab form the System Properties property sheet.

- Click device manager button.

- Select View | Devices by connection.

- Observe the hierarchy of attached device that forms the device tree.

Chapter 8

USB Drivers

USB Drivers

Objectives

After completing this unit you will be able to:

- Understand the programming architecture of the USB.

- Write a function driver for a USB device.

- Experience the hot plug & play feature of the USB.

Getting Started

- To be able to write a function driver for a USB device we must know the programming architecture of the USB.

- The programming architecture of USB includes concepts like

  - A hierarchical model for attaching devices to a computer.

  - A standard for self-identification that relies on a hierarchy of descriptors on board of the hardware.

  - A scheme for subdividing fixed-duration frames into packets that convey data to and from devices.

USB Device Connection

- The USB bus features a hierarchical model for connection of devices. The figure illustrates this hierarchical model.

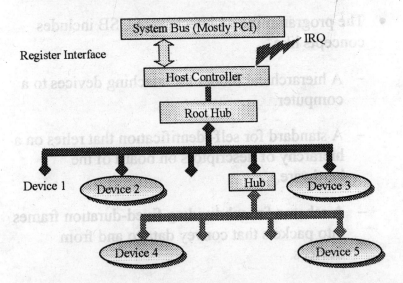

- A host controller device connects to the system bus just like any other I/O devices.

  - The OS communicates with the host controller by means of I/O ports or memory registers.

  - The OS receives event notifications from the host controller through an ordinary interrupt signal.

USB Device Connection (Cont'd)

- The host controller in turn connects to a tree of USB devices.

  - Host controllers follow one of the two standard specifications namely the Open Host Controller Interface (OHCI) or the Universal Host Controller Interface (UHCI).

- A hub serves as a connection point for other devices.

  - A root hub connects to the host controller and provides ports where devices can get connected.

  - Additional hubs can get connected to the root hub and provide for more device to get connected to the USB system.

  - Hubs can be daisy-chained together to a maximum depth defined by the USB specification.

  - Other kinds of devices, such as cameras, mice, keyboards, and so on, plug into hubs.

  - USB architecture uses the term function to describe a device that isn't a hub.

- Up to a maximum of 127 devices get connected at a time to the USB system.

- Device driver software is required for the host controller, the hub and the individual devices in the USB system.

  - Usually, the OS provides drivers for the host controller and the hub device.

USB Device

- USB devices often have one or more configurations that govern how it behaves.

  - A common reason to use more than one configuration relates to the OS. For example, a device can have a simple configuration that the system BIOS uses and a more complex configuration that the Windows driver uses.

  - The following figure shows a USB device having two configurations.

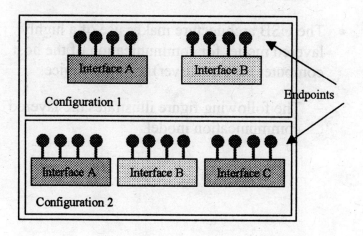

USB Device (Cont'd)

- Each configuration of a device embodies one or more interfaces that prescribe how software should access the hardware.

  - A device interface exposes one or more endpoints.

  - Each of the endpoints of an interface serves as a terminus for a communications pipe.

  - Client software communicates with the devices through these pipes.

- The USB architecture makes use of a highly layered model for communication of the host computer (device driver) with the device.

  - The following figure illustrates the layered communication model.

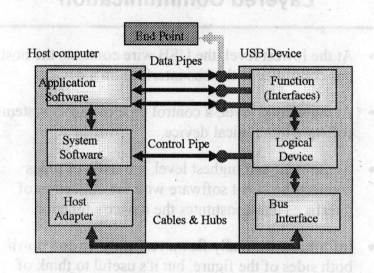

Layered Communication

- At the lowest level, the USB wire connects the host bus controller to the bus interface on a device.

- At the second level, a control pipe connects system software to a logical device.

- At the third and highest level, a bundle of pipes connect the client software with the collection of interfaces that constitutes the device's function.

- Information actually flows vertically up and down both sides of the figure, but it's useful to think of the pipes as carrying information horizontally between the corresponding layers.

- A set of drivers provided by Microsoft occupies the lower edge of the system software box in the figure.

  - These drivers include a host controller driver (**OPENHCI.SYS or UHCD.SYS**), a hub driver (**USBHUB.SYS**), and a class driver used by the controller driver (**USBD.SYS**).

  - All of these drivers are collectively often referred to as the **USBD**.

- Collectively, these drivers manage the hardware connection and the mechanics of communicating over the various pipes.

Layered Communication (Cont'd)

- WDM drivers occupy the upper edge of the system software box.

  - The job of a WDM driver is to translate requests from client software into transactions that **USBD** can carry out.

  - Drivers for USB devices never directly communicate with the device using HAL services instead they communicate with the bus driver to get work done.

  - Client software deals with the actual functionality of the device.

USB Data Flow Model

- The figure illustrates how the data sent by the client applications reach the USB device.

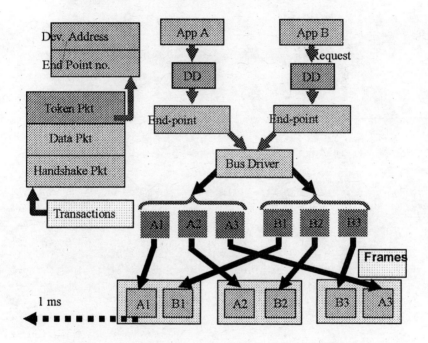

- A client program sends or receives data over a USB pipe.

  - It achieves this by calling API functions that ultimately causes the function driver for the USB device to receive an IRP.

- The driver's job is to direct the client request into a pipe ending at the appropriate endpoint on the device.

USB Data Flow Model (Cont'd)

- The driver submits the requests to the bus driver.

  - The bus driver breaks the requests into transactions.

  - The bus driver schedules the transactions for presentation to the hardware.

- Information flows on the bus in frames that occur once every millisecond.

  - The bus driver must correlate the duration of all outstanding transactions so as to fit them into frames.

- In USB, a transaction has one or more phases.

  - A phase is a token, data, or handshake packet.

  - Depending on the type, a transaction consists of a token phase, an optional data phase, and an optional handshake phase, as shown in the figure.

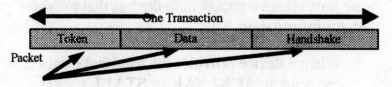

One Transaction

| Token | Data | Handshake |

Packet

USB Data Flow Model (Cont'd)

- During the token phase, the host transmits a packet of data to all currently configured devices.

  - The token packet includes a device address and (often) an endpoint number.

  - Only the addressed device will process the transaction.

  - Devices neither read nor write data on the bus for the duration of transactions addressed to other devices.

- During the data phase, data is placed on the bus.

  - For output transactions, the host puts data on the bus and the addressed device consumes it.

  - For input transactions, the roles are reversed and the device places data onto the bus for consumption by the host.

- During the handshake phase, either the device or the host places a packet onto the bus that provides status information.

  - When a device provides the handshake packet, it can send an **ACK**, **NAK** or **STALL** packet.

- **ACK** packet is send as an acknowledgment against a successful receipt of information.

- **NAK** packet is send to indicate that the device is busy and didn't attempt to receive information.

- A **STALL** packet is send to indicate that the transaction was correctly received but logically invalid in some way.

Auto Recognition Support

- USB devices maintain onboard data structures known as descriptors to allow for self-identification to host software.

- The following table shows the different types of descriptors that a device can have.

Descriptor Type	Describes
Device	An entire device
Configuration	One of the configurations of a device
Interface	One of the interfaces that's part of a configuration
Endpoint	Describes one of the endpoints belonging to an interface
String	Contains a human-readable Unicode string describing the device, a configuration, an interface, or an endpoint
Configuration	Describes capabilities of a device
Interface power	Describes power-management capabilities of a device

- Each device has a single device descriptor that identifies the device to host software.

- The host uses a **GET_DESCRIPTOR** control transaction directed to endpoint **0** to read this descriptor.

Device Addressing

- When a USB device first comes on line, it responds to a default address.

  - The default address happens to be numerically equal to zero.

- Certain electrical signaling occurs to alert the host bus driver that a new device has arrived on the scene.

  - The bus driver assigns a device address and sends a control transaction to tell "device number zero" what its real address is.

  - From then on, the device answers only to the real address.

Writing A USB Driver

- We propose to build a USB function driver for a USB device.

  - The driver would perform the minimal amount of work required to qualify as a function driver.

  - The minimal function driver is required to configure and de-configure the device as need.

- Any USB device can be used for testing this driver.

  - The only technical information need is the **product-id** and the **vendor-id** of the device.

  - This information can be obtained by using the USB Verifier utility found in the DDK.

- To obtain the **product-id** and vendor-id of the device simply follow the steps given below

  - Plug in the USB device into the root hub.

  - Fire the **USB Verifier** utility.

  - Find the device in the **USB Verifier** window and note down the **product-id** and **vendor-id** for it.

- The device used for the sample program is a USB to serial bridge control.

Writing A USB Driver (Cont'd)

- The vendor-id and product-ids are essential for the device driver to take control of the device.

  - Whenever the device is connected the PnP manager obtains the product-id and device-id from the newly attached device.

  - The PnP manager then and searches for the corresponding driver for the device based on these IDs.

  - If the driver is found it is loaded otherwise the PnP manger prompts for the location of the driver.

- Figure show the USB Verifier tool with the Prolific USB-to-Serial device connected to port1 on the root hub of the Universal Host controller.

  - The device has vendor-id 067Bh and product-id 2303h.

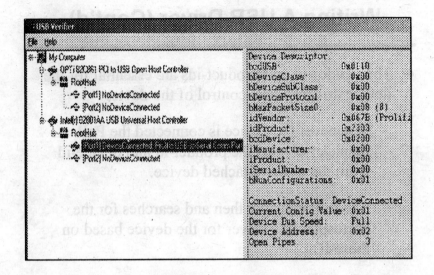

Code Example

- The code snippets of the driver are discussed in the following sections.

- The complete listing for the code example can be found in the *Chap07\minusb* directory on the CD.

Handling PnP

- The driver handles the plug and play requests sent by the plug and play manager by implementing a dispatch routine for the IRP_MJ_PNP.

- The driver only handles the following minor plug and play codes

  - IRP_MN_START_DEVICE
    IRP_MN_STOP_DEVICE
    IRP_MN_REMOVE_DEVICE

  - All other plug and play codes are passed on to the lower layered driver i.e. the bus driver.

- The code for the dispatch routine is shown below.

```
NTSTATUS DispPnp(PDEVICE_OBJECT pfdo, PIRP pIrp)
{
    DEV_EXT* pdx = ( DEV_EXT* ) pfdo->DeviceExtension ;
    PIO_STACK_LOCATION pIrpStack=
            IoGetCurrentIrpStackLocation ( pIrp ) ;
    NTSTATUS status ;
    switch ( pIrpStack->MinorFunction )
    {
            case IRP_MN_START_DEVICE :
                    status =  StartDev ( pfdo, pIrp ) ;
                    break ;
            case IRP_MN_STOP_DEVICE :
                    status = StopDev ( pfdo, pIrp ) ;
                    break ;
```

```
                    case IRP_MN_REMOVE_DEVICE :
                         status = RemoveDev ( pfdo, plrp ) ;
                         break ;
                default :
                         IoSkipCurrentIrpStackLocation ( plrp ) ;
                         status = IoCallDriver (
                                      pdx->pLowerDevObj,plrp ) ;
        }
    return status ;
}
```

Starting The Device

- Starting a USB device requires a the following steps

- Reading the device descriptor:

    - The device descriptor provides a lot of information regarding the device. Some of that information includes the following

    - String indicating the name of the device manufacturer, string indicating the name of the product, string indicating the serial number of the device, integer indicating the number of configurations supported by the device.

    - The code snippet used for reading the device descriptor is shown below

    ```
    URB urb ;
    UsbBuildGetDescriptorRequest ( &urb,
    sizeof ( _URB_CONTROL_DESCRIPTOR_REQUEST ),
    USB_DEVICE_DESCRIPTOR_TYPE, 0, 0, &pdx->dd, NULL,
    sizeof ( pdx->dd ), NULL ) ;

    NTSTATUS status = SendUrb ( pfdo, &urb ) ;
    ```

    - The code builds a USB Request Block by using the *UsbBuildGetDescriptorRequest( )* service provided by the USBD.

- Next the URB is sent to the USBD (lower layered driver) by using the user defined function **SendUrb( )**.

Starting The Device (Cont'd)

- Reading the configuration descriptor.

    - Reading the configuration descriptor requires
      two steps.

    - The first step reads the fixed-size configuration
      descriptor. The code for achieving this is shown
      below

    ```
    _USB_CONFIGURATION_DESCRIPTOR tcd ;
    UsbBuildGetDescriptorRequest ( &urb,
        sizeof ( _URB_CONTROL_DESCRIPTOR_REQUEST ),
        USB_CONFIGURATION_DESCRIPTOR_TYPE,0, 0, &tcd,
        NULL, sizeof ( tcd ), NULL ) ;

    status = SendUrb ( pfdo, &urb ) ;
    ```

    - The second step reads the configuration
      descriptor plus all embedded interface and
      endpoint descriptors. The code to achieve this is
      shown below.

    ```
    ULONG size = tcd.wTotalLength ;

    USB_CONFIGURATION_DESCRIPTOR pcd =
    ( PUSB_CONFIGURATION_DESCRIPTOR )
    ExAllocatePool ( NonPagedPool, size ) ;

    UsbBuildGetDescriptorRequest(&urb,
    ```

```
        sizeof ( _URB_CONTROL_DESCRIPTOR_REQUEST ),
   USB_CONFIGURATION_DESCRIPTOR_TYPE,0, 0, pcd,
   NULL, size, NULL ) ;

   status = SendUrb ( pfdo, &urb ) ;
```

Starting The Device (Cont'd)

- Note that the code is same as that for reading
  fixed length configuration descriptor except for
  the fact that it specifies a different size
  parameter in the call to
  UsbBuildGetDescriptorRequest( ) service.

- Configure the device by selecting a configuration.

  - The device needs to be configured by sending a
    URB that specifies the configuration to use.

  - If the device driver fails to configure the device
    then the I/O manager subsequently unloads the
    driver from memory.

  - Firstly, we need to search for the configuration
    descriptor in the list of all configuration
    descriptors supported by the device and obtain a
    pointer to an interface that matches the given
    configuration descriptor.

```
PUSB_INTERFACE_DESCRIPTOR pid =
USBD_ParseConfigurationDescriptorEx ( pcd, pcd,-1,
-1, -1, -1, -1 ) ;
if ( !pid )
{
    DbgPrint ( "minusb: No interface for device\n" ) ;
    return STATUS_DEVICE_CONFIGURATION_ERROR ;
}
```

- The searching can be accomplished by calling the *USBD_ParseConfigurationDescriptorEx( )* service.

- The first parameter specifies the address of the configuration descriptor structure and the second parameter specifies the address within the first structure from the point where searching should begin.

Starting The Device (Cont'd)

- By specifying the same parameter for first and second parameter the searching can begin from the very beginning.

- *USBD_CreateConfigurationRequestEx( )* service helps build a URB that can be sent to the host controller driver (HCD) to set the device in a configured state. The code snippet for achieving this is shown below.

```
USBD_INTERFACE_LIST_ENTRY interfaces[2] =
{
        { pid, NULL },
        { NULL, NULL },
};
PURB selurb = USBD_CreateConfigurationRequestEx (
                pcd, interfaces ) ;
status = SendUrb ( pfdo, selurb ) ;
```

- The URB is finally sent using the *SendUrb( )* user defined function.

Stopping The Device

- Stopping the device requires the following steps

- Un-configure the device:

  - The device can be un-configured by simply sending a **"select configuration"** request to the bus driver and passing a NULL parameter as the new configuration value.

```
URB urb ;
UsbBuildSelectConfigurationRequest ( &urb,
    sizeof ( _URB_SELECT_CONFIGURATION ), NULL ) ;

NTSTATUS status = SendUrb ( pfdo, &urb ) ;
```

Sending URB To Bus Driver

- The *SendUrb( )* user defined function helps to send USB Request Packets (URB) to the bus driver.

- To send the URB following steps are required

- Call the Internal Device Io Control method to pass the URB to the bus driver.

  - Internal Device Io Control is used since the one driver wants to privately communicate with another driver. Note that a client application cannot directly use the Internal Device Io Control mechanism.

  - The IOCTL code for submitting the URB to the bus driver (USBD) is **IOCTL_INTERNAL_USB_SUBMIT_URB.**

  - The InternalDeviceIoControl can be called using the *IoBuildDeviceIoControlRequest( )* service of the I/O manager.

- *IoBuildDeviceIoControlRequest( )* returns a pointer
- to an IRP with the next-lower driver's I/O stack location partially set up from the supplied parameters.

- – The returned pointer is NULL if an IRP cannot be allocated.

- – The URB has to be actually copied to the stack location for the IRP.

- • The code for the function is shown below.

Sending URB To Bus Driver

(Cont'd)

```
NTSTATUS SendUrb ( PDEVICE_OBJECT pfdo, PURB urb )
{
    NTSTATUS status ;

    DEV_EXT* pdx = ( DEV_EXT* ) pfdo->DeviceExtension ;
    KEVENT event ;
    KeInitializeEvent ( &event, NotificationEvent, FALSE ) ;
    IO_STATUS_BLOCK iostatus ;
    PIRP Irp = IoBuildDeviceIoControlRequest (
            IOCTL_INTERNAL_USB_SUBMIT_URB,
            pdx->pLowerDevObj, NULL, 0, NULL, 0, TRUE,
            &event, &iostatus ) ;

    if ( !Irp )
        return STATUS_INSUFFICIENT_RESOURCES ;

    PIO_STACK_LOCATION stack ;
    stack = IoGetNextIrpStackLocation ( Irp ) ;
    stack->Parameters.Others.Argument1 = ( PVOID ) urb ;
    status = IoCallDriver ( pdx->pLowerDevObj, Irp ) ;
    if ( status == STATUS_PENDING )
    {
            KeWaitForSingleObject ( &event, Executive,
                        KernelMode, FALSE, NULL ) ;
            status = iostatus.Status ;

    }
    return status ;
}
```

Sending URB To Bus Driver (Cont'd)

- The bus driver sends the URB to the device asynchronously.

  - When the bus driver is called using *IoCallDriver( )* it immediately returns a pending status back to indicate that the IRP processing is pending and is not completed.

  - To wait for the URB to reach the device we must use an event signaling mechanism.

  - A kernel notification event object is used for this purpose.

- Firstly the event object is initialized using the *KeInitializeEvent( )* service provided by the kernel.

  - The *KeInitializeEvent( )* service requires 3 parameters.

  - The first parameter is the address of the kernel event object to be initialized, the second parameter specifies the type of the event notification / synchronization and the third specifies the initial state of the event object signaled (TRUE) / non-signaled (FALSE).

- A non-signaled notification event is sent to the bus driver while calling the Internal device Io control method.

- The function driver then waits for the URB to reach the device by performing a wait operation on the event using *KeWaitForSingleObject( )* service of the kernel.

- Note that the wait is performed in executive kernel mode.

- The bus driver signals the event whenever the URB packet reaches the device.

Building The Driver

- The USB driver requires some changes in the sources file.

  - A USB driver utilizes the services of the **USBD** and hence requires to be linked with **USBD.LIB**.

  - The updated sources file is shown below.

```
TARGETNAME = minusb
TARGETTYPE = DRIVER
TARGETPATH = obj
TARGETLIBS = $(DDK_LIB_PATH)\usbd.lib
SOURCES  = minusb.cpp str.cpp
```

Deploying The Driver

- The Windows Driver Model requires that driver be installed via driver installation (INF) files.

  - Writing driver installation files is a topic in itself and is covered in the next chapter "Driver Installation".

  - For the time being, a **minusb.inf** file is provided in the **Chap08\minusb** directory on the CD.

- To test the driver plug in the USB device and follow the steps mentioned below

  - When prompted for the .INF file browse for the **minusb.inf** file.

  - When prompted browse for the **minusb.sys** file

  - Check out the debug messages in the kernel debugger window.

  - Unplug the device and verify that the *RemoveDev( )* and *Unload( )* routines got invoked by finding the corresponding debug messages in the kernel debugger window.

  - A reboot is not required for plugging and unplugging the device, which very clearly explains the hot plug and play support in the USB.

Summary

- Devices get hierarchically connected to the USB.

- The host controller unit connects the USB to the system bus.

- A hub device serves as a connection point for other devices.

- USB devices often support multiple configurations

- Each configuration of a device has one or more interfaces that prescribe how software should access the hardware.

- Interfaces have endpoints that serve as the terminal point of a communication pipe.

- Client applications communicate with USB devices via pipes.

- USB device drivers never directly communicate with the device instead they send requests in the form of USB request packets (URB) to the bus driver.

- The USB bus driver (USBD) breaks the request in the form of transactions and finally sends it to the physical bus.

- USB devices maintain onboard data structures known as descriptors to allow for self-identification to host software.

Lab 8

Experience Hot plug ability feature of USB

Put *Dbgrint( )* calls in every function in the driver program discussed in the chapter and observe the sequence of the output while plugging-in and removing the device.

Detailed instructions are contained in the Lab 8 write-up at the end of the chapter.

Suggested time: 60 minutes

Answers Directory: Chap08\minusb

Files: minusb.cpp, str.cpp, str.h, makefile, sources, minusb.inf

Instructions:

- Create the driver program, the sources and makefile.

- Insert *DbgPrint( )* calls with suitable messages in all the functions of the driver.

- Build the driver.

- Plug in a sample USB device.

- When prompted for browse the **minusb.inf** file provided in the **Chap08\minusb** directory

- Watch the debug messages in the kernel debugger window.

- Similarly remove the device and note the debug messages.

- Note that the addition and removal of devices does not require a reboot since the USB supports hot plug and play feature.

Chapter 9

Driver Installation

Driver Installation

Objectives

After completing this unit you will be able to:

- Understand how device drivers are installed.

- Understand the structure of INF files.

- Understand the commonly used sections and directives in an INF file.

Getting Started

- Building drivers is only a part of the story; it is equally important to make sure that the driver gets correctly installed on the end users system.

- Using registry script (.reg file) for installing drivers is not technically incorrect but this approach requires some operations to be carried out manually.

  - Registry script does not support copying of **.sys** files to the driver's directory so copying of files has to be carried out manually.

  - The installation required for Windows 98 and 2000/XP is a little different and the registry script does not provide any facility for checking the OS version or taking runtime decisions.

- Windows Driver Model (WDM) mandates that drivers use a text file with the file extension INF for driver installation.

  - The INF file controls most of the activities associated with installing drivers.

  - The INF files provides support for making registry entries, and executing different actions depending upon the version of the OS.

- This chapter discusses the INF file and several other aspects of installing drivers.

Providing The INF File

- Usually the device driver writer provides the INF file.

  - The INF file either goes on a diskette or on a disc that is packaged with the hardware.

  - Microsoft provides INF files for a lot of popula: hardware devices and puts then on the OS installation disc.

- The INF file helps instruct the OS to carry out certain operations like

  - Copying files to end user's hard disk.

  - Adding / modifying registry entries.

  - The names of the files to be copied and names of the registry entries are specified as a part of the INF file

Structure Of INF File

- An INF file is a text file organized into named sections.

  - Some sections have system-defined names and some sections have names determined by the writer of the INF.

  - Each section contains section-specific entries, which are interpreted by setup software.

  - Some entries begin with a predefined keyword. These entries are called directives.

- Some INF entries are essentially pointers from one section to another, for a specific purpose.

  - For example, an **AddReg** directive identifies a section containing entries that instruct setup to modify the registry.

  - These types of entries sometimes include additional arguments (required or optional) for setup to interpret during installation.

- Other INF entries do not point to other sections, but simply supply information that Setup uses during installation.

– The information includes filenames, registry values, hardware configuration information, flags, and so on.

– For example, the **DriverVer** directive supplies driver version information.

Structure Of INF File (Cont'd)

- An INF file contains a collection of sections introduced by a section name in brackets.

  - Most sections contain a series of directives of the form **"keyword = value"**.

- The INF file can be thought of as the linear description of a tree structure.

  - Each section is a node in the tree, and each directive is a pointer to another section.

  - Figure shows the tree structure of an INF file.

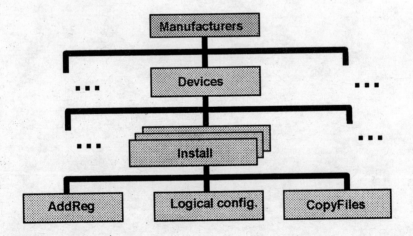

- The various sections of the INF files are discussed
  further in the chapter.

Syntax Rules For INF Files

- While writing INF files once must follow certain rules so that the setup software can properly interpret the contents of the INF files.

  - These rules cover entities like the format of section names, using string tokens, line format, continuation, and comments.

- The following rules must be observed for creating section names.

  - **Sections can be specified in any order**: Most INF files list sections in a particular order, by convention, but setup finds sections by name, not by location within the INF file.

  - Each section in an INF begins with the section name enclosed in brackets ([ ]). The section name can be system-defined or INF-writer-defined.

  - **Section names should not exceed its maximum length**: A section name has a maximum length of 255 bytes on NT-based OS. On Windows 98/Me section names can have a maximum length of 28 characters.

- INF files designed to work on both platforms must adhere to the smaller limit.

- Each section ends at the beginning of a new **[section-name]** or at the end-of-file mark.

- If more than one section in an INF has the same name, the system merges their entries and directives into a single section.

Syntax Rules For INF Files (Cont'd)

- Section names, entries, and directives are case-insensitive.

- A section name cannot contain certain characters

  - A section name referenced by a section entry or directive cannot have leading or trailing spaces, a linefeed character, a return character, or any invisible control character, and it should not contain tabs.

  - In addition, a section name cannot contain either of the bracket ([ ]) characters, a single percent (%) character, a semicolon (;), or any internal double quotation marks (") characters, and it cannot have a backslash (\) as its last character.

  - Most of these restrictions can be overridden if the section name is quoted with a "".

  - A quoted section name however cannot contain the closing bracket (]).

- Many values in an INF, including INF writer defined section names, can be expressed as string key tokens of the form *%strkey%*.

- In the INF **Strings** section of the INF file, each string key must be associated with a string value consisting of a sequence of explicitly visible characters.

- The setup code converts the strings, if necessary, into Unicode.

Syntax Rules For INF Files (Cont'd)

- Each entry and directive in a section ends with a return or linefeed character.

- The backslash character (\) can be used as an explicit line continuator in an entry or directive.

  - If part of an entry or directive, such as a path, includes a backslash at the end of a line, that backslash must be delimited with double quotation marks ("\") to override its interpretation as a line continuator.

- Comments begin with a semicolon character.

  - The setup software ignores everything that appears to the right of the *";"* character till the end of the line.

- Commas separate the values supplied in section entries and directives.

  - An INF entry or directive can omit an optional value in the middle of a list of values, but the commas must remain.

  - INF files for NT-bases systems can omit trailing commas, but Windows 9x INF files must not.

- Dual-OS INF files should specify trailing commas in any sections that are used on Windows 9x machines.

- Dual-OS INF files can omit trailing commas in sections that are only used for NT-based systems.

Syntax Rules For INF Files (Cont'd)

- A Windows 9x/Me INF file cannot be larger than 64 kilobytes.

  - There is no practical limit to the size of an INF file for NT-based systems.

  - The maximum length of a field (including NULL character) can be of 512 characters.

The Version Section

- The INF file begins with a *Version* section that identifies the type of device described by entries in the file.

  - Every INF file must have the Version section. By convention, the **Version** section appears first in INF files.

  - The following script shows an example version section.

```
[Version]
Signature = $CHICAGO$
Class = Sample
ClassGuid = {894A7460-A033-11d2-821E-444553540000}
```

  - **Signature**, **Class** and **ClassGuid** are directives specified in the version section.

- The signature directive indicates the OS for which the INF is valid.

  - The syntax of the signature directive is **Signature = "signature-name".**

  - The signature values have the following meanings.

Signature Value	Meaning
$Windows NT$	NT-based operating systems
$Windows 95$	Windows 9x/Me
$Chicago$	All Windows operating systems

The Version Section (Cont'd)

- – The enclosing $'s are required but these strings are case-insensitive.

- – If signature-name is none of these string values, the file is not accepted as a valid INF.

- Setup does not differentiate among the different signature values.

  - – However, it is recommended that an appropriate value must be specified so that someone reading an INF file can determine the OS for which the driver is intended.

- *Class* directive identifies the class of device.

  - – The syntax for Class directive is **Class = "class-name"**.

  - – Table shows the INF class name for a few standard devices.

INF class name	Description
Ports	Serial and parallel ports
USB	USB host controllers and hubs
Mouse	Mouse and other pointing devices
Modem	Modems
Keyboard	Keyboards
HDC	Hard disk controllers
CDROM	CD-ROM drives (SCSI and IDE)

- If an INF specifies a **Class** directive it should also specify the corresponding system-defined GUID value for its **ClassGUID** entry.

The Version Section (Cont'd)

- If the device does not fit into any standard device class then a new class can be created.

  - A unique, case-insensitive class-name value should be supplied that is different from any of the system-supplied classes.

  - The length of the class-name string must be **32** characters or less.

- ClassGuid uniquely identifies the device class.

  - The syntax for **ClassGuid** directive is ClassGuid = {nnnnnnnn-nnnn-nnnn-nnnn-nnnnnnnnnnnn}

  - For example the mouse device would use a statement as shown below

  - ClassGUID = {4D36E96F-E325-11CE-BFC1-08002BE10318}

  - The GUIDs for various devices are documented in the DDK.

  - If a new device class was specified then the INF file must specify a newly generated GUID value for the **ClassGUID** entry.

- New GUID value can be generated using the **guidgen** utility found in the Platform SDK.

The Version Section (Cont'd)

- A production INF file should also have *DriverVer* and *CatalogFile* directives in the *Version* section.

  - The OS will accept INF files that lack these details, but Microsoft does not certify the driver package without these statements.

- The *DriverVer* directory specifies version information for drivers installed by this INF file.

  - The syntax for the directive is
    DriverVer = mm/dd/yyyy[,x.y.v.z]

  - This x, y, v, z values specifies an optional version number.

  - If a value is specified, w is required but x, y, z, and their preceding period characters are optional.

  - If specified, w, x, y, and z must each be an integer that is greater than zero but less than 65535.

  - The value is for display purposes only (for example, in the Device Manager). The OS does not use this value for driver selection.

- The *CatlogFile* directive specifies a catalog (.cat) file to be included on the distribution media of a device/driver.

  - Catalog files are supplied by the Microsoft Windows Hardware Quality Lab (WHQL), after WHQL has tested, certified, and assigned digital signatures to driver files.

The Version Section (Cont'd)

- The digital signature for the drivers assures that the driver is designed to work perfectly with windows.

- The syntax for the directive is

  CatalogFile = filename.cat

The Manufacturer Section

- The *Manufacturer* section identifies the manufacturer of one or more devices that can be installed using the INF file.

  - Each entry in the **Manufacturer** section is known as **manufacturer-identifier** directive.

  - **Manufacturer-identifier** directive uniquely identifies a manufacturer and a section (model section) containing information that identifies a manufacturer's device models.

  - Each **manufacturer-identifier** entry must exist on a separate line and use the following format

    Manufactuer name = models-section-name

  - A sample manufacturer section is shown below

    ```
    [manufacturer]
    "Kanetkar's ICIT" = KICIT
    "Object Innovations" = OI

    [KICIT]
    ...

    [OI]
    ...
    ```

The Models Section

- Entries in the *Models* section

  - Identifies at least one device

  - References the Installation section (**DDInstall**) for the device.

  - Specifies a unique hardware identifier for the device.

- Each entry in a Models section is sometimes called a driver-node and has the following syntax

  device-description=install-section-name,hw-id[,compatible-id...]

  - **device-description** is a human-readable description of the device.

  - The **install-section-name** parameter identifies another section of the INF file that contains instructions for installing the software for a particular device.

  - **hw-id** specifies a vendor-defined hardware ID string that identifies a device, which the PnP Manager uses to find an INF-file match for the device.

Hardware ID Formats

- A hardware ID can be specified in one of the following formats

- enumerator\enumerator-specific-device-id

  - It is the typical format for individual PnP devices reported to the PnP Manager by a single enumerator.

  - For example, **USB\VID_045E&PID_00B** identifies the Microsoft HID keyboard device on a USB bus.

  - Depending on the enumerator, such a specification can even include the device's hardware revision number as, for example, **PCI\VEN_1011&DEV_002&SUBSYS_00000 000&REV_0**.

- *enumerator-specific-device-id

  - The asterisk (*) indicates that more than one enumerator supports the device.

  - For example, **PNP0F01** identifies the Microsoft serial mouse, which also has a compatible-id specification of **SERENUM\PNP0F01**.

- Entries in the Models section can also can specify one or more additional device Ids

    - These additional device Ids identify additional hardware models that are compatible with the device designated by the initial hardware ID and are controlled by the same drivers.

Hardware ID Formats (Cont'd)

- Device class specific id is an I/O bus-specific format and the exact format is described in the hardware specification for the bus.

- For true Plug and Play devices, the device identifier that appears in a manufacturer's model section of an INF is very important.

  - Plug and Play devices are those that can electronically announce their presence and identity.

- A bus enumerator can find these devices automatically, and it can read some sort of onboard information to find out what kind each device is.

  - Universal serial bus (USB) devices, for example, include vendor and product identification codes in their device descriptors.

  - The configuration space of Peripheral Component Interconnect (PCI) devices includes vendor and product codes.

- When an enumerator detects a device, it constructs a list of device identification strings.

- One entry in the list is a complete identification of the device.

- This entry will end up naming the hardware key in the registry.

- Additional entries in the list are "compatible" identifiers.

Hardware ID Formats (Cont'd)

- The PnP Manager uses all of the identifiers in the list when it tries to match a device to an INF file.

- Enumerators place more specific identifiers ahead of less specific identifiers so that vendors can supply specific drivers that will be found in preference to more general drivers.

- The algorithm for constructing the strings depends on the enumerator, as follows:

- The full device identifier for PCI devices has the form

  PCI\VEN_vvvv&DEV_dddd&SUBSYS_ssssssss&REV_rr

  - **vvvv** is the vendor identifier that the PCI Special Interest Group assigned to the manufacturer of the card

  - **dddd** is the device identifier that the manufacturer assigned to the card

  - **ssssssss** is the subsystem id (often zero) reported by the card

  - **rr** is the revision number.

- The complete device identifier for an USB Devices is

  USB\VID_vvvv&PID_dddd&REV_rrrr

  - **vvvv** is the 4-digit hexadecimal vendor code assigned by the USB committee to the vendor

  - **dddd** is the 4-digit hexadecimal product code assigned to the device by the vendor

  - **rrrr** is the revision code.

Hardware ID Formats (Cont'd)

- A single device can have more than one hw-id value.

  - The PnP Manager uses each such hw-id value, which is usually provided by the underlying bus when it enumerates its child devices

  - The Plug and Play manger creates a subkey for each such device in the **HKEY_LOCAL_MACHINE\SYSTEM\Curr entControlSet\Enum** branch of the registry.

  - For manually installed devices, the system's setup program uses their hw-id values as specified in their respective INF files to create each such registry subkey.

Device Identification

- The information in the Manufacturer section and in the model section(s) for individual manufacturers comes into play when the system needs to install a driver for a piece of hardware.

  - A Plug and Play (PnP) device announces its presence and identity electronically.

  - A bus driver detects it automatically and constructs a device identifier using onboard data.

  - The system then attempts to locate preinstalled INF files that describe that particular device.

  - INF files reside in the INF subdirectory of the Windows directory.

  - If the system can't find a suitable INF file, it asks the end user to specify one.

- A legacy device can't announce its own presence or identity.

  - The end-user therefore launches the add hardware wizard to install a legacy device and helps the wizard locate the right INF file.

The Install Section

- An install section contains the actual instructions that the installer needs to install software for a device.

  - The install section can be restricted to a particular platform by suffixing a suitable string to the install section name.

  - For example **[install-section-name.nt]** indicates that the section is only meant for NT platforms.

- The device installer looks for the install section having the most specialized suffix.

  - Table shows the install section suffixes for each platform.

Platform	Install Section Suffix
Any	**None**
NT	**.nt**
NT on x86 System	**.ntx86**
NT on Intel 64-bit processor	**.ntia64**

- The *install* section can contain many directives that are used for carrying out many of the operations required for installation the device.

- The *CopyFiles* directive can be used to copy files from the installation disc to the end users hard disk.

The Install Section (Cont'd)

- The **CopyFile** directive references one or more INF-writer-defined sections in the INF that specify a list of files to be copied from the source media to the destination.

  - The statements in a **CopyFiles** section have the following syntax:

  [file-list-section]
  destination[,source][,temporary][,flag]
  ...

  - **Destination** is the name of the file as it will eventually exist on the end user system.

  - **Source** is the name of the file as it exists on the distribution media. If the source is same as destination it's can be left blank.

  - **Temporary** specifies the name of a temporary file to be created in the copy operation if a file of the same name on the destination is open or currently in use. This parameter is only used on Windows 9x/Me platforms.

  - The Flags parameter contains a bit mask that governs whether the system will decompress a file and how the system deals with situations in which a file by the same name already exists.

Creating The Driver Service

- A device driver needs a service entry in the SCM database for getting loaded.

  - The Service section in the INF file controls the creation/deletion of services.

  - The Service section name is indicated by appending the ".**Services**" keyword to the install section name

  - For example if the install section name is **DriverInstall.NT** then the corresponding services section name would be **DriverInstall.NT.Services**.

- The *AddService* directive facilitates creates of service entries.

  - The **AddService** has the following general syntax

  AddService = ServiceName,[flags], service-install-section

  - **ServiceName** specifies the name of the service to be installed.

- **flags** specifies as a hexadecimal value that governs whether the different service entries in the registry have to be overwritten or not.

- **service-install-section** references an INF-writer-defined section that contains information for installing the named service for the device.

Creating The Driver Service
(Cont'd)

- The service-install-section has a lot of directives. Some of these directives are shown below.

```
[service-install-section]

[DisplayName=name]
[Description=description-string]
ServiceType=type-code
StartType=start-code
ErrorControl=error-control-level
ServiceBinary=path-to-service
```

  - A service-install-section has at least the **ServiceType**, **StartType**, **ErrorControl**, and **ServiceBinary** entries, all other entries are optional.

  - **DisplayName** directive specifies a friendly name for the driver usually expressed as a %strkey% token defined in a **Strings** section of the INF file.

  - Description directive optionally specifies a string that describes the service, usually expressed as a %strkey% token defined in a Strings section of the INF file.

- – This **description** string gives the user more
  information about the service than the
  DisplayName.

Creating The Driver Service
(Cont'd)

- If a description-string contains any %strkey% tokens, each token can represent a maximum of 511 characters.

- The total string, after any string token substitutions, should be no longer than 1024 characters.

• The ServiceType value for the driver should be 1

  - The value 1 is equivalent to the constant SERVICE_KERNEL_DRIVER

• The *StartType* specifies when the driver has to be started. The following tables shows the possible values.

Start Type value	Description
0	**SERVICE_BOOT_START**
1	**SERVICE_SYSTEM_START**
2	**SERVICE_AUTO_START**
3	**SERVICE_DEMAND_START**
4	**SERVICE_DISABLED**

- **SERVICE_BOOT_START** value must be used for drivers of devices required for loading the OS.

- **SERVICE_SYSTEM_START** indicates a driver started during OS initialization.

- PnP drivers that do device detection during initialization but are not required to load the system should use this value.

Creating The Driver Service (Cont'd)

- **SERVICE_AUTO_START** indicates a driver started by the Service Control Manager (SCM) during system startup.

- This value should never be used in the INF files for WDM or PnP device drivers.

- **SERVICE_DEMAND_START** indicates a driver started on demand, either by the PnP Manager when the corresponding device is enumerated or possibly by the Service Control Manager in response to an explicit user demand for a non-PnP device.

- This value should be used in the INF files for all WDM drivers of devices that are not required to load the system and for all PnP device drivers that are neither required to load the system nor engaged in device detection.

- **SERVICE_DISABLED** indicates a driver that cannot be started.

- This value can be used to temporarily disable the driver services for a device.

Creating The Driver Service (Cont'd)

- *ErrorControl* specifies the level of error control that has to be performed if the driver is fails to load or initialize.

  - The following tables shows the possible **ErrorControl** values

StartType value	Description
0	SERVICE_ERROR_IGNORE
1	SERVICE_ERROR_NORMAL
2	SERVICE_ERROR_SEVERE
3	SERVICE_ERROR_CRITICAL
4	**SERVICE_DISABLED**

  - **SERVICE_ERROR_IGNORE** indicates that system startup should proceed with system startup and do not display a warning to the user.

  - **SERVICE_ERROR_NORMAL** indicates that system startup should proceed but display a warning to the user.

- **SERVICE_ERROR_SEVERE** indicates that system startup should switch to the registry's **LastKnownGood** control set and continue system startup, even if the driver again indicates a loading or device/driver initialization error.

- **SERVICE_ERROR_CRITICAL** indicates that system startup is not using the registry's **LastKnownGood** control set, switch to **LastKnownGood** and try again.

- If startup still fails when using **LastKnownGood**, run a bug-check routine.

Creating The Driver Service
(Cont'd)

- Only devices/drivers necessary for the system to boot specify this value in their INF files.

- **ServiceBinary** specifies the path to the binary for the service, expressed as **%dirid%\filename**.

- The **dirid** number is one of the system-defined directory identifiers.

- The most commonly used value for **dirid** is **10**, which refers to **\system32\drivers** directory.

Tools for INF Files

- Creating an INF file from scratch is a difficult but not impossible job.

- The DDK provides a few tools for creating and managing INF files.

  - The GenInf.exe tool is useful for creating of a new INF file.

  - The **Chkinf.bat** help to validate the syntax of an INF file.

- GenINF.exe is a GUI-based tool that guides the user through the process of creating INF files.

  - The application features a INF File Creation Wizard that significantly reduces the time taken for creation of INF files

- The GenINF tool however has a lot of restrictions

  - The **GenINF** does not generate fully valid INF files it only generates a skeleton of INF files

  - Device driver deplorers need to modify the generated INFF file and modify it as required.

- **GenINF** supports all device classes, but includes specific support for only certain device classes.

- **GenINF** is located in the \Tools subdirectory of the DDK installation directory.

- **GenINF** supports the creation of INF files for Windows® 2000 only. It does not create INF files for Microsoft Windows 95, Windows 98, or Windows NT 4.0.

Tools for INF Files (Cont'd)

- The *ChkINF* tool is actually a Perl script that checks the structure and syntax of .inf files.

  - The ChkINF produces results in HTML format.

  - The HTML file includes a list of the errors and warnings detected in each .inf file, with each error and warning shown next to the errant .inf file entry.

  - The ChkINF tool includes support for all .inf sections and directives that apply to all classes of devices.

  - The tool in located in the Tools directory of the DDK, and should be executed from an MS-DOS Command prompt.

Summary

- WDM drivers get installed using a text-based file that has an .INF extension.

- INF file is organized in section and directives.

- A pair of square brackets surrounds section names.

- Some of the sections are standard and some are defined by the INF file creator

- Entries in the sections are known as directives and follow the general form **"keyword = value"**.

- A device ID present in the INF file uniquely identifies a piece of hardware.

- The PnP manager build a device ID from the data available on the device and scans for the corresponding INF file.

- The GENINF tool can be used to create a INF file

- The CHKINF tool can be used to check the validity of the INF file.

Lab 9

Creating INF File

Create an INF file for the USB function driver developed in chapter 8 using the GENINF utility in the DDK.

Detailed instructions are contained in the Lab 9 write-up at the end of the chapter.

Suggested time: 60 minutes

Answers Directory: Chap08\minusb

Files: usbfunc.inf, sample.inf, minusb.sys

Instructions:

- Start GENINF.EXE from the tools directory of the DDK.

- Follow the steps of the wizard and fill suitable information for the USB device.

- Name the inf file as usbfunc.inf.

- Click Finish.

- Compare the contents of the sample.inf file with the generated inf file (usbfunc.inf) and accordingly make the necessary changes.

- In particular a classinstall32 section has to be added to the GENINF created file.

- Deploy the USB function driver in chapter 8 using usbfunc.inf.

522   Writing Windows Device Drivers

Driver Testing and Debugging

Objectives

- After completing this chapter, you will be able to:

Chapter 10

Driver Testing and Debugging

Driver Testing and Debugging

Objectives

After completing this unit you will be able to:

- Understand how device drivers are tested.

- Understand the testing & debugging environment of device drivers.

- Understand and read crash screens

- Analyze a crash dump.

Getting Started

- As we already know Device Drivers programs run at kernel level and are highly trusted by the OS.

- A badly written or errant device driver can wreck havoc on the system.

  - For example, an unhanded exception in a device driver can result in a system crash.

  - Sometimes, the crash results in an unrecoverable situation.

- Therefore it is highly necessary for device driver writers to thoroughly test the device driver code before distributing it.

  - To find out bugs and errors one might need to test and debug drivers.

  - Debugging a driver requires that debugging at the kernel level using a kernel mode debugger.

- The chapter discusses the methods and tools used for testing and debugging device driver code.

WHQL Certification

- Hardware and drivers must pass WHQL testing to receive a "Designed for Windows" logo.

    - Designed for Windows logo helps in assuring the end-user that the hardware and its corresponding driver are tested by Microsoft to work perfectly with windows OS.

    - Device manufacturers can license the Windows Logo for use on product packaging, advertising, and other marketing materials for all systems and components that pass compliance testing.

    - WHQL stands for Microsoft's **Windows Hardware Quality Labs**.

    - WHQL tests drivers for compliance with requirements of the Windows Logo Program for hardware.

- WHQL certified hardware and drivers additionally avail the following benefits

    - WHQL certified drivers receive a digital signature in the form of a catalog file (**.cat**). Digital signature plays a very important role in d iver installation. The setup program normally blocks the installation of non-digitally signed driver.

– WHQL approved hardware and drivers are included on the **Hardware Compatibility List (HCL)** site.

– WHQL approved drivers are distributed as part of the **Windows Update** program.

WHQL Certification (Cont'd)

- Drivers need to be thoroughly tested before being submitted to the WHQL.

  - The DDK includes a tool called **Driver Verifier** for testing device drivers.

  - The WHQL also provide some software test programs that can be downloaded from **www.microsoft.com/hwtest**.

  - The WHQL provided test programs tests the working of both hardware device and software.

Checked Vs. Free Build OS

- Microsoft provides a checked build and a free build of the OS.

- The free build is the same as the build of the OS that is sold to customers.

  - The free build is sometimes referred to as the retail build.

  - The system and drivers are built with full optimization, and debugging asserts are disabled.

  - Performance tuning, final testing, and verification of the driver should be done on the free build.

  - The faster speed of the free build makes it possible to detect race conditions and other synchronization problems.

  - The free build of the OS is built with full compiler optimizations.

  - If the free build discovers correctable problems, it continues to run.

- Distribution media containing the free build of the OS do not have any special designation.

Checked Vs. Free Build OS (Cont'd)

- The checked build serves as a testing and debugging aid for both the OS and for kernel-mode drivers.

  - The checked build of the OS is created specifically to make identifying and diagnosing OS-level problems easier.

  - The checked build contains extra error checking, argument verification, and debugging information that is not available in the free build.

  - Bugs and problems in device driver code can be isolated and tracked down much more quickly than on a free build.

  - Additional debugging code in the checked build protects against many driver errors.

  - A checked build of the system and drivers is larger and slower, and uses more memory, than the free build.

  - The checked build of the OS has many compiler optimizations disabled. Disabling such optimizations makes it easier to understand disassembled machine instructions, and therefore easier to trace the cause of problems in system software.

– The checked build also enables a large number of debugging cross checks in the OS code and system-provided drivers. This helps the checked build identify internal inconsistencies and problems as soon as they occur.

– Distribution media containing the checked build are labeled "Debug/Checked Build."

Checked Build OS

- The checked build distribution contains

  - Checked version of the OS code, checked HALs, checked drivers, checked versions of the file systems and checked (debug) builds of many of the user-mode components.

- The checked build includes a significant number of debugging "cross-checks" that are normally not present in the system. These checks include:

  - **Parameter validation checks:**

  - Great care has been taken to ensure that the Windows OS code ordinarily executes with as little overhead as possible.

  - As a result, the NT-based OS implement the policy that all components running in kernel-mode, including drivers, implicitly "trust" each other.

  - Parameters that are passed from one kernel-mode component to another (such as parameters passed on function calls) are typically subject to minimal validation

- Internal checks for OS correctness and consistency

- These checks typically verify the correctness of key algorithms and data structures in the OS.

- Checks of this type may also be inserted by one of the Windows developers during the OS debugging process to help isolate difficult problems.

Checked Build OS (Cont'd)

- Informational checks and tracing output

  - These checks, and the resulting output that is displayed in the debugger, are designed to assist debugging of drivers or other system-level components.

  - The existence of such checks and their debug output may vary from release to release of the OS.

Driver Verifier

- Driver Verifier is a tool that can monitor kernel-mode drivers to verify that they are not making illegal function calls or causing system corruption.

  - It can perform a large number of checks on drivers, as well as subject them to a variety of stresses and tests to flush out improper behavior.

  - Driver Verifier can be used on any number of drivers simultaneously, or on one driver at a time.

  - It has various options that can be enabled or disabled. This allows putting a driver through heavy stresses or through a more streamlined test.

  - Driver Verifier works on both the free and checked builds of OS.

  - The driver Verifier is present in the tools directory of the DDK.

  - The following screen capture shows the interface provided by the driver verifier utility.

Driver Verifier (Cont'd)

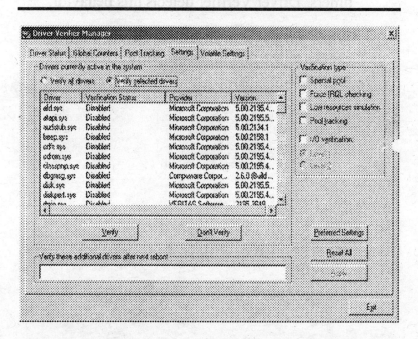

- Some of the features of the Driver Verifier are discussed below.

- Automatic Checks

  - These checks are always performed on a driver that is being verified, regardless of which options have been selected.

  - If the driver uses memory at an improper IRQL, improperly calls or releases spin locks and memory allocations, improperly switches stacks, or frees memory pool without first removing timers, Driver Verifier detects this behavior.

- When the driver is unloaded, Driver Verifier checks to see that it has properly released its resources.

Driver Verifier (Cont'd)

- Special Memory Pool

    - When this option is active, Driver Verifier allocates most of the driver's memory requests from a special pool.

    - This special pool is monitored for memory overruns, memory under-runs, and memory that is accessed after it is freed.

- Forcing IRQL Checking

    - When this option is active, Driver Verifier places extreme memory pressure on the driver by invalidating pageable code.

    - If the driver attempts to access paged memory at the wrong IRQL or while holding a spin lock, Driver Verifier detects this behavior.

- Low Resources Simulation

    - When this option is active, Driver Verifier randomly fails pool allocation requests and other resource requests.

- By injecting these allocation faults into the system, Driver Verifier tests the driver's ability to cope with a low-resource situation.

- Memory Pool Tracking

  - When this option is active, Driver Verifier checks to see if the driver has freed all its memory allocations when it is unloaded.

  - This reveals any memory leaks present in the driver code.

Driver Verifier (Cont'd)

- I/O Verification

  - When this option is active, Driver Verifier allocates the driver's IRPs from a special pool, and monitors the driver's I/O handling.

  - This detects illegal or inconsistent use of I/O routines.

- Automatic Checks

- Driver Verifier performs the following actions whenever it is verifying one or more drivers regardless of the individual options.

- Monitoring IRQL and Memory Routines

  - Driver Verifier monitors the selected driver for the following forbidden actions:

  - Raising IRQL by calling *KeLowerIrql( )*.

  - Lowering IRQL by calling *KeRaiseIrql( )*.

  - Requesting a size zero memory allocation

  - Allocating or freeing paged pool at an IRQL above **APC_LEVEL**.

- Allocating or freeing non-paged pool at an IRQL above **DISPATCH_LEVEL**.

- Trying to free an address that was not returned from a previous allocation

- Trying to free an address that was already freed

Driver Verifier (Cont'd)

- Acquiring or releasing a fast mutex at an IRQL above **APC_LEVEL**.

- Acquiring or releasing a spin lock at an IRQL other than **DISPATCH_LEVEL**.

- Double-releasing a spin lock.

- Specifying an illegal or random (un-initialized) parameter to any one of several APIs.

- Marking an allocation request **MUST_SUCCEED**. No such requests are ever permissible.

- If Driver Verifier is not active, these violations might not cause an immediate system crash in all cases.

- Driver Verifier monitors the driver's behavior and issues bug check 0xC4 if any of these violations occur.

- Monitoring Stack Switching

  - Driver Verifier monitors stack usage by the driver being verified.

- If the driver switches its stack, and the new stack is neither a thread stack nor a DPC stack, then a bug check is issued.

- This will be bug check 0xC4 with the first parameter equal to 0x90.

- The stack displayed by the **KB** debugger command will usually reveal the driver that performed this operation.

Driver Verifier (Cont'd)

- Checking Freed Pool for Timers

  - Driver Verifier examines all memory pool freed by the driver being verified.

  - If any timers remain in this pool, bug check 0xC7 is issued.

  - Forgotten timers can eventually lead to system crashes that are notoriously difficult to account for.

- Checking on Driver Unload

  - After a driver that is being verified unloads, Driver Verifier performs several checks to make sure that the driver has cleaned up.

  - In particular, Driver Verifier looks for:
    Undeleted timers
    Pending deferred procedure calls (DPCs)
    Undeleted look-aside lists
    Undeleted worker threads
    Undeleted queues
    Other similar resources

  - Problems such as these can potentially cause system bug checks to be issued a while after the driver unloads, and the cause of these bug checks can be hard to determine.

- When Driver Verifier is active, such violations will result in bug check 0xC7 being issued immediately after the driver is unloaded.

Testing Drivers

- The following are some suggestions that may be used for building and testing of device drivers.

  - Use **GenINF** utility to create a skeleton INF.

  - Always use INF files for deploying and testing drivers.

  - Use the **ChkINF** tool to verify the structure and syntax of the INF file, and to assist in diagnosing INF and other installation related issues.

  - Use **Driver Verifier** to test the code implementation of the driver.

  - Test the driver and device on as many different hardware configurations as possibly.

  - Varying the hardware can help to find conflicts between devices and other errors in device interactions.

  - Test the driver and device on multiprocessor systems.

  - Use both the free build and the checked build of the target OS.

Driver Debug Environment

- To be able to debug device driver one needs to understand the driver debug environment, which involves understanding the following concepts.

  - Hardware and software requirements for debugging.

  - Debug symbol files.

  - System Crash

  - Reasons for system crash

  - Crash-dump files.

  - Enabling crash dumps on the target system.

  - Analyzing crash dump files

  - Enabling the target system's debug client.

  - Overview of debugging routines

- The standard Microsoft tools for debugging device drivers require that two systems be used a host and target.

- The purpose of this section is to describe the details required to successfully set up this debugging environment.

H/W & S/W Requirements

- Debugging a kernel-mode driver requires two machines, a target computer and a host computer.

  - The target machine executes the driver under test.

  - The host machine, sometimes referred to as the development system, runs the debugger (e.g. **WinDbg**) and therefore controls the operation of the target.

  - The two machines are connected together using a null-modem serial cable.

  - The following figure shows the typical setup for debugging a kernel-mode driver.

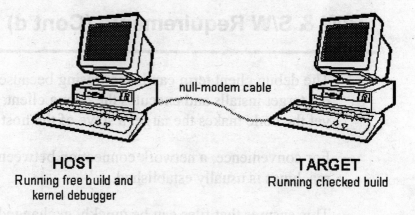

HOST
Running free build and
kernel debugger

TARGET
Running checked build

- An important but confusing term is debug client.

    - The target machine must be booted into a special environment whereby it installs the debug client between the serial port and its OS code.

    - The debug client is the small block of code that allows the host debugger, via the serial port, to control the operation of the target system.

H/W & S/W Requirements (Cont'd)

- The debug client term can be confusing because the target installs and executes the debug client, yet the code makes the target a slave of the host.

- For convenience, a network connection between machines is usually established.

- This ensures that files can be quickly exchanged - providing that both machines are operational.

- Note that while the target is paused by **WinDbg**, it cannot participate in network operations.

• Host system

- The host system is typically used to compile and link the test driver, and it runs **WinDbg** kernel debugger.

- The list of software that a host should contain
  Windows 2000 Retail build
  Visual C++
  Platform SDK
  Windows 2000 DDK
  Symbol files for target OS build
  Driver source code
  Driver symbol file(s)

- The host does not necessarily need to execute the same OS version as the target, but having the same OS is more convenient.

- The host requires the symbol file for the OS version running on the target.

H/W & S/W Requirements (Cont'd)

- Target System

    - The target system provides the execution environment for the test driver.

    - It is typically configured with the following:
    Windows 2000 retail and checked builds with debugging enabled for both
    Driver executable (e.g .SYS file)
    Driver hardware
    Full crash dump enabled
    Some tools from the Platform SDK (e.g. **WinObj**)
    Hardware compatibility tests (HCTs) from the DDK.

- As explained later in this chapter, the boot.ini file on the target must be configured to allow selection of the appropriate windows 2000 kernel (retail or checked).

    - The checked version runs with considerable assertion and debug code enabled (at the cost of reduced OS performance).

- The extra code can produce intermediate output that is helpful for tracing some driver or driver-related bugs.

- Connecting the host and target

  - To debug a driver interactively with **WinDbg** the host and target must be connected using serial ports on each machine.

  - A standard null-modem cable can be used.

H/W & S/W Requirements (Cont'd)

- Since COM ports come in two flavors of connectors, DB-9 and DB-25 (both male on the computer), a dual-headed cable Y DB-9 or DB-25 female connectors at each end) is the preferred accessory.

- Table shows the necessary connections.

DB9/DB25 connector	Signal	DB9 / DB25 connector
2	Transmit to Receive	3
3	Receive To Transmit	2
7	Ground	7

Debug Symbol Files

- One of the more puzzling aspects of debugging is the role of symbol files.

  - Symbol files contain symbolic names of entities like function and variable names.

  - The symbol files are useful in the process of debugging. The debugger makes use of the symbol files to correctly display the name of the function / variable.

  - Symbol files falls into two categories OS and driver.

- Operating System Symbols

  - With the release of each version (i.e., service pack) of Windows 2000, Microsoft releases the public symbols for that build.

  - Public symbols are essentially the information that could have been extracted from the linker's load map, except that they are in debugger-readable format.

  - The information is read, used, and displayed by the debugger during a stack trace operation, a

trace or step operation, or when evaluating and
setting breakpoints.

– Microsoft does not publish private symbol
  information for its OS.

– Such information is deemed proprietary, and
  unless a bug were being chased in the OS itself,
  it is not particularly helpful.

Debug Symbol Files (Cont'd)

- The public symbol information however is quite useful and is a recommended installation for application as well as driver debugging.

- OS symbols are unique to each build (service pack) of an

- Always install the symbols for the base OS first by using the Windows 2000 customer Support Diagnostics CD. Then after a service pack is applied to the OS, locate symbol file for the service pack (the location varies based on the update is obtained) and install it over the existing OS symbols.

- By default, OS symbols install into a directory **%SystemRoot%\Symbols**.

- The debugger must point to appropriate directories for a given debug session.

- For **WinDbg**, the symbol path can be configured from the Options dialog of the View menu, Symbols tab.

- Driver Symbols

- The driver symbols are created when the driver source compiles and links.

- The symbols for a driver (as for the OS itself) fall into public and private categories.

- The public symbols provided link map information (correlating function names and addresses),

Debug Symbol Files (Cont'd)

- The private symbols information includes source-line linkages, data type definitions, e.g. **typedefs** and **static** declaration (functions and data).

- To generate public symbol information for a driver, the link switch **/pdb:"filename"** can be used.

- To generate private symbol information, the compiler switch **/Zi** is used.

- As with the OS symbol data, the debugger must be informed of the path of the driver symbol data.

System Crash

- When Microsoft Windows encounters a condition that compromises safe system operation, the system halts.

  - This condition is called a bug check.

  - It is also commonly referred to as a system crash, a kernel error, or a Stop error.

  - If crash dumps are enabled on the system, a crash dump file is created.

  - If a kernel debugger is attached and active, the system causes a break so the debugger can be used to investigate the crash.

  - If no debugger is attached, a blue text screen appears with information about the error.

  - This screen is called a blue screen, a bug check screen, or a Stop screen.

- The exact appearance of the blue screen depends on the cause of the error. The following is an example of one possible blue screen:

```
STOP: 0x00000079 (0x00000002, 0x00000001, 0x00000002,
0x00000000)
Mismatched kernel and hal image.
```

Beginning dump of physical memory
Physical memory dump complete. Contact your system
administrator or technical support group.

System Crash (Cont'd)

- Every system crash is identified via a unique bug check code.

  - The bug check code is the very first number after the STOP word.

  - Each bug check code has four associated parameters.

  - The meaning of associated parameters change with each bug check code.

  - A description for the bug check code and the meaning of the associated parameters can be found in the DDK documentation.

- Bug checks can occur for a variety of reasons including the following

  - Un-handled exception from kernel mode.

  - Accessing paged out memory while running at or above DPC Dispatch IRQL level.

  - A driver explicitly requested a bug check by using the *KeBugCheck( )* or *KeBugCheckEx( )* service.

System Crash (Cont'd)

- When a kernel-mode error occurs, the default behavior of Microsoft Windows is to display the blue screen with bug check data.

- However, there are several alternative behaviors that can be selected:

  - A memory dump file can be written.

  - The system can automatically reboot.

  - A memory dump file can be written, and the system can automatically reboot afterwards.

  - A kernel debugger (such as WinDbg) can be contacted.

- When a fatal kernel error occurs on an NT-based OS, Windows will halt the system and attempt to locate a kernel debugger.

- If no debugger is currently attached, a blue text screen appears with information about the error.

  - This halting of the system is known as a bug check.

- It is also sometimes referred to as a Stop error, a kernel error, a system crash, or a blue screen.

System Crash (Cont'd)

- There are three different varieties of crash dump files.

  - Complete Memory Dump

  - Kernel Memory Dump

  - Small Memory Dump

- The difference between these dump files is one of size.

  - The Complete Memory Dump is the largest and contains the most information, Kernel Memory Dump is somewhat smaller, and the Small Memory Dump is only 64 KB in size.

- To enable this feature on a target machine, the following steps are required.

  - From the control panel, select the system applet.

  - Select the advanced tab and choose the startup and recovery button. The following dialog pops up.

System Crash (Cont'd)

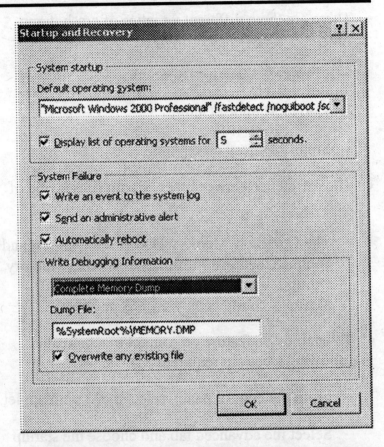

- Select either complete memory dump or kernel memory dump from the write debugging information group and select OK.

- Reboot the system, as the change made to this reconfiguration take effect only with the next boot.

- When a crash occurs, the system copies an image of physical memory into the paging file of the root partition.

- During the next boot, the image is copied into the file specified with Control Panel.

System Crash (Cont'd)

- Forcing a memory dump with a keystroke sequence

  - By modifying a registry entry, windows 2000 allows the user to generate a keystroke sequence, ctrl-scroll lock (twice) to force a system stop with the message.

  - After the system has halted a memory dump occurs and the system reboots.

  ***STOP: 0x000000E2 (0x0000000, 0x0000000, 0x00000000)
  The end-user manually generated the crashdump.

  - The registry entry is located in the key HKLM\System\CurrentControlSet\Services\i80 42prt\Parameters.

  - By adding the value with the name, type, and data shown below, the feature is enabled.

Value Name	Data Type	Value
CrashOnCtrlScroll	REG_DWORD	1

  - This often turns out to be useful for generating a .dmp file.

Analyzing the Crash Dump File

- *WinDbg* can analyze kernel-mode memory dump files.

  - To analyze a dump file, start **WinDbg**.

  - Open a crash dump file by selecting the **File | Open Crash Dump** menu command.

  - When the **Open Crash Dump** dialog box appears, use the dialog box to select the proper path and file name. When the proper file has been chosen, click **Open**.

  - Dump file can also be opened after the debugger is running by using **.opendump** (Open Dump File) command, followed with **G** (Go).

  - Dump files generally end with the extension *.dmp* or *.mdmp*.

- Analysis of a dump file is similar to analysis of a live debugging session.

  - Once the kernel debugger gets connected to the .dmp file it displays a prompt.

  - Now one can execute kernel debugger commands to query the state of the OS when the

OS crashed in order to analyze and figure out the reason for the crash.

– Note that it is not necessary that the crash dump file should be opened on the target machine. Any machine can be used for crash dump analysis.

Enabling Debug Client

- The retail and checked versions of windows 2000 include a debugging client.

  - The debugging client allows the kernel to communicate over a serial line with the WinDbg debugger.

  - The debug client must be enabled on the target system during the boot process.

- To enable the debug client, select the OS for the target machine with cursor keys while the system boot screen is displayed Press F8 and select (with cursor keys) the option for Debugging mode.

  - Press Enter Twice to boot the system.

  - By default, the debug client uses the **COM2** port, configured for **19200** baud.

  - These are the same defaults used by **WinDbg**.

  - To use a different port or baud rate, the BOOT.INI file located on the boot partition root must be modified.

Modifying Boot.INI

- Booting under NT based OS makes use of the boot.ini file.

  - Boot.ini file controls the boot options, the debug options, and many other features.

  - The file is located on the root directory of the first bootable partition of the first physical driver of the system.

- The boot.ini file is organized into sections and directives similar to an .INF file.

  - Sections are names marked in a pair of square brackets

  - The directives are of the form key = value.

- The boot.ini file is a read-only hidden file located on the boot partition's root directory.

  - To edit it, the system, hidden and read only attributes must be removed.

  - Then the file is modified using any familiar test editor, such as notepad.

- The file is similar in structure to an INF file and contains a section labeled **[operating systems]**.

- Each entry (line) within this section is displayed on the system boot screen as a choice for user selection.

- A timeout value located in the **[boot loader]** section specifies how long the user has to make this choice.

Modifying Boot.INI (Cont'd)

- The format of each line of the **[operating systems]** section includes an ARC –style path to the specific drive, partition and directory, which holds kernel files.

- An = "description" value specifies the text shown to the user on the boot screen for the selection.

- An example, of a BOOT.INI file is

```
[boot loader]
timeout=30
default=multi(0)disk(0)rdisk(0)partition(2)\WINNT

[operating systems]
multi(0)disk(0)rdisk(0)partition(2)\WINNT="w2k pro" /fastdetect
C:\="Microsoft Window"
```

- To specify a boot option for debugging, switches are added to an existing or new *[operating systems]* entry.

  - The relevant switches for debugging are listed in the following table.

Option	Description
/DEBUG	**Enables kernel debug client**
/NODEBUG	**Disables debug client (default)**
/DEBUGPORT=PortName	**Specifies COMn port to use**
/BAUDRATE=BaudRate	**Specifies baud rate for COM port**
/CRASHDEBUG	**Causes debugger to activate only upon system bugcheck**
/SOS	**Displays list of modules loaded while system starts**
/MAXMEM=MB Size	**Specifies maximum memory available to this boot.**

Modifying Boot.INI (Cont'd)

- An example entry to allow the user to select a debug client on COM port 4, with abaud rate of 38.4 Kbaud, would be

Multi(0)disk(0)rdisk(0)partition(2)\WiNNT="W2K Debug"
/debugport=COM4 /bauderate=38400

- If two different kernels are installed on the same system, they must reside in different directories.

- The **[operating systems]** entry would specify the appropriate directory instead of WINNT.

Debugging Routines

- Special debugging routines are available for kernel-mode drivers that aid in the debugging process.

  - These routines facilitate sending of messages to the kernel debugger and allow setting of breakpoints.

  - The debugging code in the driver can be conditionally compiled against the **DBG** preprocessor flag.

  - If the driver is build by running the Build utility from the **Checked Build Environment**, the **DBG** flag will equal **1**.

  - If driver is build by running the **Build** utility from the **Free Build Environment** window, **DBG** will equal **0**.

- The following sections summarize the kernel mode debugging routines

  - Routines named *DbgXxx( )* are kernel-mode routines that can be used in either free or checked drivers.

- Routines named *KdXxx( )* are kernel-mode macros that are defined only if the **DBG** flag is set.

- The *KdXxx( )* routines are active only in a checked build of a driver.

- Sending Output to the Debugger

  - *DbgPrint( )* displays output in the debugger window.

  - This routine supports the basic *printf( )* format parameters.

  - Only kernel-mode drivers can call *DbgPrint( )*.

Debugging Routines (Cont'd)

- Breaking Into the Debugger

  - When a kernel-mode program breaks into the debugger, the entire OS freezes until the kernel debugger allows execution to resume.

  - If no kernel debugger is present, this is treated as a bug check.

  - *DbgBreakPointWithStatus( )* also causes a break, but it additionally sends a 32-bit status code to the debugger.

  - *KdBreakPoint( )* & *KdBreakPointWithStatus( )* are the checked versions of these routines.

- Conditionally Breaking Into the Debugger

  - Two conditional break routines are available for kernel-mode drivers.

  - These routines test a logical expression. If the expression is false, execution halts and the debugger becomes active.

  - The **ASSERT** macro causes the debugger to display the failed expression and its location in the program.

- The **ASSERTMSG** macro is similar, but allows
an additional message to be sent to the
debugger.

- These two macros take effect only if the code is
compiled in the **checked build environment**
and the resulting driver is then run on a checked
build.

Summary

- Driver testing and debugging is important since drivers are a trusted piece of software and an errant or ill behaved driver can easily cause the system to crash.

- The *Driver Verifier* utility in the DDK can be used to test the driver.

- The *CHKINF* utility in the DDK checks the syntax of the INF file.

- The *WinDbg* kernel debugger is used for debugging drivers.

- A system crash is also known as bug check.

- Every system crash has a unique bug check code along with 4 associated parameters.

- The checked build of OS runs slowly but helps identify and report errors to a larger extent than the retail build of the OS.

Lab 10

Analysis of Crash Dump

Generate a crash dump file by pressing Ctrl + Scroll Lock (twice). Using WinDbg perform an analysis of the crash dump file.

Detailed instructions are contained in the Lab 10 write-up at the end of the chapter.

Suggested time: 45 minutes

Instructions:

- Establish a remote debugging session.

- Use the .crash command in WinDbg to explicitly crash the target m/c.

- Copy the resulting .dmp file to the host machine.

- Open the dump file in WinDbg debugger using File | Open Crash Dump menu option

- Obtain the status of the crashed machine using the following commands:

  .bugcheck – displays the bug check code that

caused the crash

.cxr – displays the current execution context

Notes